WAIT TILL YOU SEE THE BUTTERFLY

WAIT TILL YOU SEE THE
BUTTERFLY

AND OTHER SHORT STORIES
FOR BOYS AND GIRLS

Doreen Tamminga

THE BANNER OF TRUTH TRUST

THE BANNER OF TRUTH TRUST

3 Murrayfield Road, Edinburgh EH12 6EL, UK
P.O. Box 621, Carlisle, PA 17013, USA

*

© Doreen Tamminga 2010

ISBN-13: 978 1 84871 101 3

*

Typeset in 11/15 Adobe Garamond Pro at
the Banner of Truth Trust, Edinburgh

Printed in the U.S.A. by
Versa Press, Inc.,
East Peoria, IL

 CONTENTS

INTERMEDIATE READERS (7–9)

OLDEST READERS (10–12)

Contents

 INTRODUCTION

One of my best memories as a child is of the long Sunday afternoons between church services. After lunch my brothers and sisters and I would climb on to the couch and, curled up close to Dad, enjoy one of the many children's stories he read us – stories of adventure near and far, stories of childish worries with happy endings, but always stories meant to point us to the Lord.

The stories that follow were written for children aged between 4 and 12. Stories for the youngest readers (4–6) come first, followed by stories for middle readers (7–9), ending with stories for the oldest children (10–12).

Each story is concerned with a particular issue or doctrine relevant to children's lives. The topical index at the back of the book is a useful tool for parents or teachers who are looking for stories on specific topics, such as temptation or thankfulness, self-righteousness or forgiveness, tithing or the use of time, or simply a Christmas or Easter story.

Sometimes we read to our children just for pleasure, and sometimes we do so to instruct them. These stories were written with the intent of pointing children to the Lord Jesus as the only Saviour from sin, and to encourage Christian living. I hope they will be a blessing to many young hearts.

DOREEN TAMMINGA
September 2010

1: WAIT TILL YOU SEE THE BUTTERFLY

Except a corn of wheat fall into the ground and die, it abideth alone: but if it die, it bringeth forth much fruit.
John 12:24

'Look!' Kyle breathed softly. 'It's a cocoon, Becky. A butterfly cocoon.'

'What? What is?' little Becky demanded loudly. 'I don't see it. I don't see any butterfly.' She poked her face into the bushes for a better look.

'Over here', Kyle said, lifting some leaves. 'See? Hanging from the branch by that big leaf? That yellowish thing.'

'That's not a butterfly', Becky said scornfully, with all her four-year-old wisdom. 'It's just a dead leaf or something.' And she pulled her face out of the bushes.

'No, it's not a butterfly', Kyle agreed. 'It's really a caterpillar in a cocoon that's turning into a butterfly.'

'Well if there's a caterpillar stuck in there, let's get it out', Becky suggested.

'No', said Kyle. 'It needs to stay in there, or else it won't grow into a butterfly.'

'I think that's mean', said Becky. 'You should let it out. But anyway', she called over her shoulder as she ran across the lawn, 'Caterpillars don't turn into butterflies!' She ran into the house, slamming the door behind her.

'Mom!' she called. There was no answer. Caterpillars don't turn into butterflies, do they? she thought again to herself. Kicking off her shoes, Becky ran upstairs to her room. There she picked up the jar off her desk. It had some twigs and leaves in it, and crawling on one of the leaves were two caterpillars. Becky stared at them carefully. No, they are not turning into butterflies, she decided, not the teensiest bit!

When Becky found Mom hanging laundry outside, she asked her if a caterpillar could really turn into a butterfly. Mom told her that it does. The caterpillar sheds its skin and makes a chrysalis — a cocoon — around itself and hangs from a leaf stem or branch. Then, inside the chrysalis, it slowly begins to change. The caterpillar's body changes and grows wings. After two weeks, or sometimes even a whole winter, a butterfly comes out.

Becky listened in amazement, and then ran to tell Kyle. 'Kyle! It's true!' she called. 'Caterpillars really do turn into butterflies! First they make a cocoon, and then they grow wings.'

Kyle was still peering in the bush. 'I know. That's what I told you', he answered his little sister. 'Come, look. The cocoon is almost see-through. See? You can see the wings right through it. That means the butterfly is going to come out soon; maybe tomorrow.'

Becky looked carefully, and she could see the pattern of the butterfly's wings right through the chrysalis. 'What happened to the caterpillar?' she asked Kyle. 'Did the caterpillar die?'

'No', said Kyle. 'It changed into a butterfly.'

'But where is it? Mom said it shed its skin, and now it's gone. It must be dead.'

'Not really', Kyle answered again. 'It just changed.' He thought for a moment. 'The caterpillar ended and a new insect began.'

'Too bad', Becky interrupted.

'Well, if the caterpillar had stayed a caterpillar, there would never be a butterfly.' Kyle explained. He crawled out from under the bush and stood up. 'But just wait till you see the butterfly, Becky. It will be beautiful. Then you won't mind about the caterpillar at all.'

۶ﻪ

You probably knew that butterflies came from caterpillars, didn't you? But did you ever stop before and think that for the life of a butterfly to begin, the life of a caterpillar has to end? You cannot have a new butterfly without this happening.

The Lord Jesus also had to die before He could save His people. But like Becky, His followers did not understand this. They did not want the Lord Jesus to die. They thought that He should rule on earth as a king without dying first. And so the Lord Jesus tells them about a farmer.

It is spring. The days are getting warmer, and it is time for the farmer to plant his seed. In a sack he has hundreds of smooth round kernels of wheat. And so the farmer goes out and plants the seeds. The sun shines warmly, the rain falls softly, and the seeds become warm and wet. Soon the shells around the seeds begin to soften. A little later they begin to rot. Eventually they even die and fall off.

Too bad. The farmer's seeds have all died, and he will have no wheat this year. Right? No! That's not right at all. If the seeds' shells did not soften and fall away, the wheat would not grow. The seeds must be buried in the ground and 'die'. Then the small kernels of wheat will grow tall into a great field of wheat.

This is the story that the Lord Jesus told to His followers. And what do you think He meant by it? Do you remember how the Lord Jesus also died and was buried? Too bad, His followers thought. Now the Lord Jesus cannot save His people. And were they right? No! They were not right at all. If the Lord Jesus had not died and been buried, He would not have been able to save His people. The Lord Jesus had to die, just like the kernels of wheat, so that when He rose again from the dead He could save many, many people. That is the story of Easter. From death comes new life.

&.

'Kyle! Kyle! Come quickly!' Becky shouted running into the house. 'The butterfly's coming out! I just looked under the bush and one of its wings was starting to come out.'

Kyle raced down the hall, stuffed his feet into his shoes, and ran across the lawn after his little sister. Sure enough, the butterfly was moving and breaking open the chrysalis with its wings.

'Now aren't you glad that you didn't set the caterpillar free from its cocoon?' Kyle asked his sister. 'It would never have turned into a butterfly.'

'Uh-huh', Becky agreed. 'Should we get a stick and poke the rest of the cocoon off?' she asked.

'No', Kyle answered. 'You would probably hurt the butterfly and it needs to break the cocoon with its wings to make them stronger, so that it can fly.'

In a few moments the butterfly was free and hanging upside down to dry. The children could see the beautiful pattern of orange sprinkled with white dots and outlined in black. A few more minutes passed, and the butterfly spread its wings. Out from the bush it flitted, across the lawn, then away out of sight. A new life had begun. 🦋

2: THE THUNDERSTORM

> *What time I am afraid, I will trust in thee.*
> Psalm 56:3

It was late at night. The sun had set many hours ago, and now the moon was spreading its white light over the earth below. Shining through the bare tree branches, the slowly rising moon cast lacy shadows on the ground. Sliding across the yard, it touched the blades of grass, making their tips a frosty white. Silent moonbeams glided up the side of a house and into a window.

It was a bedroom window, and two girls lay tucked snugly together in a double bed. The curtain hung partly open, forgotten in their hurry to jump into bed that night, for brrr! it was cold! Quickly they had said their prayers, and asked the Lord to keep them safely through the night, and soon they lay peacefully sleeping. They did not even notice when the moon shone its silvery light across their faces. The house was quiet and still, and Christy and Laura slept on.

Soon the wind picked up and began to blow, softly at first, then harder. The small trees swayed and the great oaks creaked beneath its force. A few forgotten leaves scattered and swirled before its breath, circling around the yard before piling up in the fence corners. Dark clouds drifted across the moon, erasing the white glow from the house and yard below.

Inside, the bedroom grew suddenly dark as though a hand had pulled the curtains closed. A low rumble of thunder was heard in the distance. Christy rolled over, pulling the blankets off Laura as she turned. Lightning streaked through the sky, and a roll of thunder answered from nearby. Laura tossed in her sleep, becoming cold without the blankets. Suddenly a flash of lightning lit up their room and a great clap of thunder 'boomed' right over the house.

Startled, the girls sat bolt upright in bed. Laura, her eyes wide and scared, scooted over close to Christy. Her older sister looked almost as frightened, staring at the window and watching for another flash of lightning. Sure enough, it came, lighting their bedroom like the flash of a camera. For a second it was silent, then another great 'boom!' sounded overhead, seeming to lift the very shingles off the roof in fright.

As the last thunderclap had drawn the girls up out of bed, this one popped them both back under the safety of the blankets. There they lay huddled and still. You would almost think they were sleeping, except for the four wide eyes that peeked from the edge of the covers. The eyes squeezed shut with the next lightning flash, and the heads suddenly disappeared. A big jump under the blankets followed the echoing thunderclap.

'Oh, Christy!' Laura's voice quavered as their heads slowly peered back out of the blankets. 'I'm so scared!'

'Me too', Christy answered her younger sister. 'I don't like thunderstorms. They're so loud and – oh!' A 'boom!' of thunder interrupted her words, and both their heads disappeared again for a moment.

'I don't like the lightning shining in our room', Laura continued. 'It seems like it wants to get us. Can you close the curtain, Christy?' she asked.

'Just face the other way so you can't see the window', Christy answered. She didn't dare to go near the window to close the curtain. 'If you face the wall, you won't be able to see the lightning', she told Laura.

'Yes, I can still see it', Laura protested. 'It shines right on the wall.' And another flash of lightning shone through the window proving her right.

Ducking her head for the 'boom!' that followed, Laura asked again. 'Can you close the curtain all the way, Christy? I don't dare to.'

And Christy, not willing to show herself a coward before her younger sister, threw back the blankets and dashed to the window. Yanking the curtains shut she hurried back and leaped into bed as another clap of thunder echoed around the house. The lightning wasn't as bright with the curtain closed, and Laura was glad for that.

The wind continued to blow, swaying the tree tops outside their window. A branch scratched at the window pane, as though trying to get in.

'It's so windy out', Laura said. 'Do you think a tree will fall down?'

'No, it's not a tornado or anything like that', Christy answered, 'but lightning could hit a tree, and then it might fall. That's what happened to Melanie in my class. A tree was hit by lightning in their yard, but it didn't fall on their house.'

'What if lightning hits one of our trees?' Laura asked. 'Or what if it hits our house?'

'I don't know', Christy answered, 'but it probably won't. We have lots of thunderstorms, and it never happened before.'

Laura thought about this, then asked Christy, 'Remember what Daddy read in the Bible at suppertime? He read about the Lord throwing the lightning down. We can ask Him not to throw it at our house.'

'The Lord doesn't really throw the lightning, Laura', Christy told her. 'That's what Josh asked Dad. The storm shoots the lightning.'

'But the Lord must still steer it', Laura protested, 'because in Sunday School our teacher said that nothing bad can happen to you unless the Lord lets it. And even if something bad happens, He will take care of you.'

Christy was silent. Finally she agreed, 'Yes, then we don't have to be afraid of the lightning or the storm, because the Lord will aim it where He wants it to go.'

'That's what our Sunday school text was!' Laura exclaimed. 'Just what you're talking about! "What time I am afraid, I will trust in thee" (*Psa.* 56:3).'

'Well, we're afraid, so that's what we should do right now; then maybe we will be able to go back to sleep', Christy answered.

'Do you think we could pray again before we go to sleep?' Laura asked her sister. 'We can ask the Lord to help us trust in Him and make us not be so scared of the lightning.'

'Yes', Christy agreed. 'And we can thank Him, because, listen! The storm is almost gone.'

And so they did. Do you think the Lord is pleased to hear the prayer of two frightened girls? 🦋

3: MUDDY TRACKS, MUDDY HEART

> *Create in me a clean heart, O God; and*
> *renew a right spirit within me.*
> Psalm 51:10

'Eww! Look at this stuff; it's all squishy!'

'Hey, let me see. That's a different kind of mud. It's not brown, it's grey!'

'Yeah, and feel it. It's sort of smushy instead of slimy.'

'Maybe it's clay! The kind of stuff that you make stuff out of. Let's dig up some more!'

The two boys were standing in the shallow creek bed that ran across their back property. Dressed in red rain boots and raincoats and armed with long sticks, they had been splashing through the water. Every so often they would stop to poke at a curious looking rock or to dig in the soft creek bottom with their sticks.

The mud they stirred up had clouded the water, making the creek a murky brown. But this time the results were different.

Muddy Tracks, Muddy Heart

Once again Gregory had been poking in the mud, but now the mud didn't stir up into a brown haze. Instead, a glob of grey came up out of the water on the end of his stick. It was Jared who decided it was not mud, but clay.

'I know!' he said suddenly. 'Let's get somethin' to put it in, and we can take some home and make something out of it.'

'Okay!' his twin brother agreed excitedly. 'There's a plastic bag stuck in that bush. We can stick it in there.'

And so Jared held the bag open while Gregory scooped lumps of wet clay from the bottom of the creek. The water was a little deeper in this part of the creek. In fact, it was about an inch deeper than their rain boots were tall, and so as much as they tried to stand on their tippy-toes, both boys soon had boots full of water. Still, Gregory continued to scoop, his wet coat sleeves slapping through the water. Streaks of brown and grey dribbled down both boys' coats and pants. Speckles of mud splattered their faces like freckles and somehow a blob of mud had even made it into Jared's hair.

'Okay, I think that's enough', said Jared as the bag became very heavy. And so they headed back to the house, the dripping bag sloshing between them. Excitedly they tromped right up the back steps, into the laundry room, and across the floor to the laundry tub where they heaved the bag in. Then, turning back to hang up their coats, they saw two tracks of mud leading across the clean linoleum straight to their feet.

The boys looked at each other.

'Uh oh', Gregory said.

They looked at the kitchen door, expecting to see Mom appear at any moment. They looked at their hands, and their coat sleeves dripping a puddle around their feet. In one movement, they hurried back to the door where they kicked off their boots and hung their coats on the hooks.

'We better wipe the floor', Jared said, 'I'll get a towel.' And he disappeared into the bathroom.

Gregory waited. 'Hey, what's taking you so long?' he finally asked when Jared didn't come back. He pushed open the bathroom door and saw Jared pushing himself up on the counter to look into the mirror.

'Look at my face!' Jared said. 'I've got freckles!' He looked at his brother. 'Ha! So have you. Come look in the mirror.'

Gregory climbed up on the counter and also looked. He grinned at the sight of a blob of mud on his head.

A door closed upstairs. Both boys stopped grinning and looked at each other. 'Mom's coming!' was their thought, and they turned the water on full force. Most of the mud seemed to leave their skin and collect on the mirror and counter and faucet. The clay was a little trickier, however. It didn't seem to want to leave their skin, and when they did scrub it loose, it clung to the sides of the sink. Taking the white hand towel off its hook, the boys dried the leftover freckles from their face and wiped the sink, leaving streaks of grey behind. They hopped off the counter and came out of the bathroom.

'Oh yeah, the floor', Gregory said.

Quickly Jared grabbed a yellow bath towel from the rack. Pushing it over the floor like a mop, he collected most of the water and dirt in the towel. Shaking it out, the boys held up the filthy towel.

'Um, I think Mom usually uses something else to clean the floor . . .' Gregory was saying when the door to the laundry room opened. Mom came in with a basket of ironing.

She stopped short at the sight of the two boys and the towel. At her look, Jared quickly lowered it and rolled it into a ball.

'We were just cleaning the floor', he said.

'I see', Mom said. 'And your pants and coat? Where have you been playing?'

'In the creek', Gregory said. 'We found some clay.'

'I see', Mom said again, and she looked past them into the bathroom at the flooded countertop, the splattered mirror and grey-streaked faucet and sink. 'I *see*', she said again.

'Um, we tried to clean it up', Jared said nervously. 'But it's kind of smeary stuff.'

'Okay', Mom told the boys. 'Listen. When you've been playing in the creek and come home filthy, pull off your boots at the back door. And if you're trying to clean off this smeary clay', she gave a puzzled look at the bag in the laundry tub, 'call me before you make a bigger mess!'

'Yes, Mom', the boys said, and Gregory added, 'We thought you'd be more mad about the mess; that's why we tried to clean it up ourselves.'

'I know', Mom said with a sigh. 'I probably would have done the same thing if I were you', she admitted. 'That's how we are. We always want to clean things up before we get in trouble. Even with God. When we've sinned, instead of going straight to Him and asking Him to wash our hearts clean, we first try to clean up our sin ourselves. But it never works, boys. It never works.'

Mom got out a rag and some cleaning solution. 'Now', she continued, 'you can do something for me while I clean up the bathroom. The recycling bin and green bin need to be emptied outside.'

'Okay! I'll get the recycling, you get the green bin', Jared told his brother, and the boys ran off, glad to be able to help.

Outside, Jared sorted the paper and tin and plastic into the different recycling bins, then headed over to the compost bin, to see what was taking Gregory so long.

Gregory had dumped the banana and apple peels and coffee grinds into the compost and was now staring into the bin. 'Hey', he said when Jared came over to peer in too. 'Do you see what colour that old orange is turning? It's kind of fuzzy white and green.'

'Sick!' said Jared fascinated. 'And look at those rotting bananas; they're covered with little bugs! It smells pretty gross too. Let's shut the lid.'

'No, wait!' Gregory stopped him. 'I want to poke it with the pitchfork first. We'll get the grass stuff on top to cover up all the gross stuff. That helps turn all this stuff into mud for the garden.' And so Gregory jabbed away in the compost pile with the pitchfork. But all his poking only revealed more layers of rotting compost. Worms wiggled through the food and grasses, and little spiders ran from the light.

'Ugh', Jared said and turned away in disgust. 'Put the cover on; it's only getting worse.'

Gregory wrinkled up his nose in agreement, and with one last jab, pulled out the pitchfork.

Coming into the house, the boys pulled off their boots at the door. The bathroom smelled fresh and lemony, and the laundry room floor was shiny clean.

'You should see what's all in the compost, Mom!' Gregory told her as she came out of the bathroom with her scrub brush. 'Everything's turning weird colours. It's disgusting!'

Mom smiled. 'I know', she said, 'but it will give us very good soil for the garden this summer.'

'Gregory was trying to cover all the yucky stuff with the grass stuff', Jared told her, 'but it only got grosser and smellier.'

'Oh, you boys', Mom said and laughed. 'Always trying to clean it up and make it better. Well, that's a good thing, I guess, but remember that it's what's inside of a person that makes a person dirty, not the outside. That's what the Lord Jesus said. You can look all nice and clean on the outside, but have a sinful dirty heart on the inside.'

'I know', Jared said, 'That's why we need a new heart.'

'That's right', Mom said, as she dumped a load of laundry into the washing machine. 'We can't clean our heart ourselves. Just like poking in the compost only made it look and smell worse, the more we try to clean up our own heart, the more sins we will uncover. There is only one who can clean our heart, and even if He's given us a new heart, we still make it dirty with sins. And so we need to ask for forgiveness, for the Lord Jesus to clean it again and again, every day.' ❧

 # 4: CANDY CRAVINGS

> *I have learned, in whatsoever state I am,*
> *therewith to be content.*
> Philippians 4:11

Brenda came skipping happily into the house. 'I'm home!' she called. Hanging her coat up, she dropped into a chair at the kitchen table. Mom was wiping down the stove and counters. Her little sister Danielle climbed up on to a chair next to her.

'How was Corrine's birthday party?' Mom asked.

'Fun!' Brenda replied. 'We played Pin-the-Tail-on-the-Donkey and Musical Chairs, and then we played Home-free Hide-and-Seek outside. They have a huge yard, and I never got caught once. Rianne was 'it' three times. Then we had pizza and ice cream for supper. And before, we had birthday cake, and she liked the books I gave her. She didn't have them yet.'

'It sounds like you were busy!' said Mom. 'Were Rachel and Karen there too?'

'Yes', Brenda answered. 'And Rianne and me.'

'I wish I could've gone too', sighed Danielle leaning her chin on her hands. 'Brenda always goes to birthday parties.' She

16

looked over at the little bag in Brenda's hands. 'Hey! Did you get a goody bag? What's in it? Can I have something?' she asked eagerly.

'There's some candy and stuff', said Brenda. 'You can have some. Here, you can have the candy necklace', she added. She knew Danielle loved candy necklaces.

'Goody!' Danielle exclaimed. 'What else is in there?'

Brenda pulled a few candies and a fun-dips package from the bag. 'I'm going to save this for later', she announced. 'I love these and grape flavour is my favourite.'

Danielle looked longingly at the fun-dips. In her mind she could imagine the smooth feel of the candy dipping stick and the sugary sweetness of the flavoured powder. She followed Brenda upstairs to the bedroom they shared and watched as Brenda put the candy in her dresser drawer. Her own candy necklace lay forgotten downstairs on the kitchen table.

'Brenda!' Mom called from the bottom of the stairs. 'You should come finish up some homework before it's time for bed.'

'Coming!' Brenda answered.

'And Danielle', Mom continued. 'Get your pyjamas on, and get ready for bed. I'll be up in a few minutes.'

'Okay', Danielle answered. She went to the dresser she shared with Brenda and pulled open the drawer to get out her pyjamas. Looking in, she saw the goody bag from the birthday party, and sticking out, the tip of the fun-dips package. Reaching into the drawer, she pulled out her pyjamas. Then, hesitating for just a moment, Danielle snatched out the fun-dips. Clutching her pyjamas in one hand, and the package in the other, she ran to the bathroom and locked the door.

A few minutes later, Mom came up and knocked on the door. 'Danielle, are you finished in there? Open the door, and I'll help you with brushing your teeth.' Slowly the door opened and two guilty eyes stared up at Mom. 'What's all that purple around your mouth?' Mom asked, getting a washcloth.

Danielle felt scared. She knew what she had done was wrong, and she was afraid of getting in trouble.

'Nothing', she lied to Mom.

'It looks like candy', Mom said, starting to wipe Danielle's face.

'What looks like candy?' Brenda asked, suddenly appearing at the bathroom door. She stared hard at her sister's mouth. 'What is all that purple around your mouth, Danielle?' she demanded. 'You ate my fun-dips!'

Danielle was even more scared. Now she was caught. 'I did not!' she exclaimed with tears in her eyes.

'Yes, you did', Brenda retorted, and she rushed over to look in the garbage. 'See! Here's the package!' Turning away, she left the bathroom and ran to her bedroom. Tears welled up in her eyes. Why had Danielle been so mean? She had shared the candy necklace with her and been nice, and this is what Danielle did back to her! Brenda sat on the edge of her bed, still holding the empty wrapper.

ও

Why had Danielle been so mean to Brenda? Why had she stolen and eaten her sister's candy?

Well, it all started when Danielle coveted Brenda's fun-dips. She saw it and wished that she had it. Brenda had already given her a candy necklace, but she wasn't happy with it anymore. She wanted more. This first sin of coveting led to another sin, stealing. And stealing led to another sin, lying. Now Brenda's happiness was gone, and so was Danielle's. She had thought that eating the fun-dips would make her happy, but instead, she was scared, sorry, and unhappy. Sin never brings the happiness we expect it to bring.

But what can we do when we have already sinned?

Tell it to the Lord, and ask Him for forgiveness. Ask Him to give you a new heart, a contented heart, one that is happy with what He has given you. When Jesus fills your heart, you will not need other things to make you happy. This is what Paul is talking about when he says: 'I have learned, in whatsoever state I am, therewith to be content' (*Phil.* 4:11). No matter what happens to him, Paul is saying, he can be happy because he has the Lord in his heart.

5: FREEDOM FOR BOOTS

> *Blessed are the undefiled in the way, who walk in*
> *the law of the LORD . . . Thou hast commanded us*
> *to keep thy precepts diligently.*
> Psalm 119:1, 4

Michael laughed as Boots grabbed his shoelaces with his sharp little teeth and pulled. With another puppy growl, Boots jerked the laces again, then tumbled backwards as he lost his grip. Bouncing back on his feet, he came bounding back, and Michael scooped him up in his arms. A warm, pink tongue licked across his chin.

Michael squeezed him tighter. Boots was the best birthday present he had ever had. Dad had said, now that Michael was ten, he was old enough to have a dog. It would be a lot of work though, Dad had warned Michael, because, just like people, puppies can have a mind of their own; they don't always listen.

Just then the back door opened and Mom stepped out on to the porch. The sun had risen above the trees and warm light stretched across the lawn to where Michael was playing with Boots. The yard was filled with brightly coloured leaves that had come down in the wind storm last night.

'Come get your lunch!' Mom called. 'It's time to go to the bus stop.'

'Okay', Michael replied and set Boots down in a pile of leaves. His tail waving furiously, the puppy squirmed out and dashed after Michael as he walked to the porch.

'Bye, Michael', Mom said and zipped up his jacket. 'Have a good day!'

Michael picked up his lunch. 'Bye, Mom.'

He turned to the puppy at his feet. 'Goodbye, Boots. I'll see you after school. Have fun!' he added as he latched the gate behind him.

Boots followed Michael to the gate and began jumping against it anxiously. Where is Michael going? he barked. Why can't I come with you? Why is there a big fence locking me in?

Boots whined and yelped. There was a big world out there to explore! Tree stumps and bicycles, garbage cans and other dogs all waited his inspection, but he couldn't get out. Finally, with one last whimper, he settled down to wait for Michael. His head resting on his paws, he didn't take his eyes off the gate.

꒰꒱

You have all heard of the Ten Commandments, haven't you? The minister reads them every Sunday. Well, who wrote these Ten Commandments? God did, you remember. He wrote them on two stone tablets and gave them to Moses on Mount Sinai. And what are these commandments? They are ten laws that God says we must obey.

These laws tell us that we must serve God only, and keep Sunday holy. We must not steal, kill or hate, or be envious of something that is not ours. God also tells us to honour our moms and dads by respecting and obeying them. And when Jesus came to earth, He explained that the most important thing for us to do is to love God, and then to love the people around us as much as we love ourselves.

Why did God make all these laws? Why can't we do what we want? Before you answer this, let's go back to Michael's back yard. There is Boots, lying forlorn behind the locked gate. And now tell me, why couldn't Boots go running loose around the neighbourhood while Michael was gone to school? Why was there a fence and a gate to keep him in the backyard? You know, don't you?

The fence was there to keep Boots safe. Outside the fence were all kinds of dangers for a puppy. The streets were filled with cars and bicycles, strangers and big dogs. A little puppy could easily get hurt or lost. So the back yard, with its sticks and bones, leaf piles and dog house, was the best place for Boots.

In the same way, God's law is like a fence for us. It keeps us from the danger of sin. Just like Boots was safest when he was kept in the yard by Michael, we are safest when we are obeying the laws of God. And even though Boots didn't understand this, Michael knew it and was doing what was best for him.

We don't always want to obey God's laws; we don't always want to be kind to others, or to listen to our parents, but God has told us that this is the best thing for us to do. Ask God for a new heart that will want to keep His commandments. And when you do break His laws, go back to God on your knees in prayer, and ask Him to forgive you for Jesus' sake.

Clang! The gate swings open and Michael runs through, dropping his schoolbag on the porch. With an excited yelp, Boots springs to his feet and hurtles through the yard, bouncing into Michael's arms. In a moment, he is back out again to race once more around the yard. He is safe and happy. How can you be safe and happy?

6: LOST AND FOUND

'Are we almost there yet?' Heidi asked Alicia for the second time.

'Yup', her big sister replied. 'We only have to walk one more block. Look for the big sign "New and Used Books".'

'I wish we could have got off the city bus right at the bookstore', Heidi said. 'My toes are frozen.'

The two girls had taken the bus into the city that afternoon. Alicia had heard of this bookstore from a friend at university. She could buy used textbooks here and save a lot of money. School started again next week, and so she had made the trip into the city today and taken her little sister, Heidi, along.

'There it is! I see the sign!' Heidi suddenly called out and ran ahead to wait by the door.

Alicia quickly caught up and the two girls hurried inside. Ah, it was so nice and warm in the store. Heidi pulled off her mittens and stuffed them in her pockets. Then she looked. And looked.

Books, books, and more books were everywhere. Shelves of them, stands of them, and racks of them were on display in front of her, beside her, and above her. Rows and rows, aisles and aisles of glossy covers, leather covers, bright covers, as far as she could see. Heidi's eyes grew big and she looked up at Alicia. Alicia looked at her face and laughed.

'Come on', she said. 'We'll take a look at the children's section before I look through the used book section.'

The two girls settled on cushioned chairs and spent a little time flipping through different storybooks and reading some picture books. Heidi found a used book called *Animals in the Bible*. She turned to the page about sheep. The story told of a lamb that was looking for better grass to eat. He wandered farther and farther away from the flock, always wanting just one more juicy bite. At last he grew tired and wanted to go back, but he had lost his way. He hurried this way and that, and finally began bleating for the shepherd. Night was falling, but before it grew dark, the shepherd found him and brought him home. Heidi stared for a moment at the picture of the shepherd carrying the tired lamb home. How kind the shepherd looked, and how safe and happy was the lamb in his arms.

Soon Alicia stretched and got up. 'I have to go pick out the textbooks I need. It shouldn't take long. Do you want to go with me, or finish off your book?'

'Will you come right back here and get me?' Heidi looked up and asked.

'Yup. Shouldn't be more than ten minutes', Alicia assured her.

'All right, then, I'll finish my book', Heidi decided and Alicia disappeared down one of the aisles.

Heidi kept turning the pages of her book, looking at all the pictures, and soon reached the end. She reached for another book, but then got up to check if Alicia was coming back yet. No, not yet. She sat down to wait. And wait. She got up and checked again. No Alicia. What was taking her so long? Heidi walked down to the end of the aisle to see if she could see her. No. No Alicia. She went back to sit and wait. And wait. Where was Alicia?

Heidi started to feel panicked. What if she didn't come back? What if Alicia couldn't find her? Without thinking, Heidi hurried back down the aisle to look. From there she went down the next aisle and the next, and then another. Just like the little lamb in the story, she hurried on farther and farther. No Alicia anywhere. Only rows of books, quiet customers, and busy sales clerks.

At last Heidi decided to go back and wait in the children's section. She started back and turned down the first aisle, or should it have been the second? She thought she had come from over here, or was it from over there? Heidi didn't know. Her heart started to pound faster and her book began to get slippery in her sweaty hands. Which way was the children's section? She wasn't lost, was she? Tears filled her eyes, but she pinched her lips shut to keep from crying. I can't be lost, she told herself.

Just then a sales clerk passed by. She paused as she saw Heidi's worried face. 'Is everything all right?' she asked kindly.

Heidi was embarrassed. She didn't want the lady to see her tears, and she was still sure she could find her way back. Quickly, she nodded.

'All right, then', the lady said and walked on. 'Just let me know if you need any help.'

With another nod, Heidi turned and went back the way she had come. On she walked, up one aisle and down the other, her eyes so full of tears that everything looked blurry. By now she wasn't so sure any more that she could find her own way back. She had to admit it. Just like the little lamb, she was lost. He had bleated out for the shepherd to come. But who could she ask for help? Past row after row of books she trudged. At last she rounded a corner and almost bumped into the same sales clerk that had spoken to her before.

'You're lost in this big bookstore, aren't you?' the lady asked again. And this time Heidi agreed with a tearful nod.

'I can't find my sister', was her whispered plea for help.

'Well, let's just go to the customer service counter and we'll find her for you', the sales clerk said kindly. Heidi clung to the lady's hand and followed her up to the counter. The sales clerk pulled out a stool and said, 'Now you just sit right here, and we'll have your sister back in no time. Now, what's your sister's name?'

Heidi sat huddled on the stool as Alicia's name was given over the loudspeaker. Timidly she turned her head to see if she could see Alicia coming. What if she didn't hear the announcement? she worried. What if she had already left the store?

And then, before another minute could pass, Heidi saw a familiar figure hurrying through the crowds. It was Alicia, looking as worried as Heidi felt. 'There you are!' she exclaimed when she saw Heidi. 'I was looking all over for you! Thank you', she added to the sales clerk. And now the tears that Heidi had been holding back came trickling down her cheeks. She was so relieved. She was so glad that she had been found. If she had been a lamb, she would have leaped for joy. Instead, she clung tightly to her sister's hand. She had been found, and she wouldn't let go again, of that she was sure.

After paying for their books, the girls headed back out into the cold. It was windy here in the city, and the cold seemed to creep right through their coats. With a shiver they hurried down the sidewalk. Snow was falling thickly and muffled the sounds of cars driving slowly by. Pedestrians hurried along, their scarves and collars drawn up close around their ears. Finally reaching the bus stop, the girls boarded the waiting bus for home.

With a groan and a creak, the bus pulled out into the traffic. Heidi pressed her nose to the cold window. It was dark outside except for the flash of white snowflakes whisking past the street-lights. Inside the bus it was warm and cosy. With a happy sigh, Heidi pulled out her new book. She turned to the story about the lamb.

'I was just like you, little lamb', she whispered to the face peeking out from the shepherd's cloak.

'Yes, you were', Alicia said, leaning over with a smile.

'The shepherd rescued this lost little lamb', Heidi explained to her sister.

'I see', Alicia said. 'Did you know that that story is an example of the Lord Jesus? He is called the Good Shepherd. We are like that lost lamb. We go skipping away in our sins, becoming more and more lost, but we pretend we know the way home. We ignore the Good Shepherd. We think that we can save ourselves, that we can make ourselves better and wash some of our own sins away. But it just gets worse and worse. We get more and more lost. If we finally realize that we are lost, we will cry out for help to the Good Shepherd. Then the Lord Jesus will hear our cry; He will rescue us and save us from our sin.'

Heidi looked out of the window into the dark. She could picture a world full of lost sinners. Did they know they were lost? And if they knew, would they cry out to the Lord Jesus? She knew He would save every single one that cried to Him. Even she herself. It gave her much to think about and much to pray about.

With another long sigh, Heidi tucked her arm through Alicia's. 'I like that story even better than the lamb's', she said.

What about you? Have you learned that you are lost in sin and that you cannot find your way back to the Lord by yourself? Cry out to the Lord for a clean heart, a heart that will love Him and not run away from His commandments. He is the Good Shepherd; He will hear your cry.

7: KEEPERS OF THE SHEEP

> *And the shepherds returned, glorifying and praising God for all the things that they had heard and seen.*
> Luke 2:20a

Jeremy leaned his head back against the seat and watched the houses speed by the window. In one hand he clutched a new Bible story book, and the other hand held a bag with an orange and some chocolate candies. Jeremy, his Mom, Dad, and two sisters were on their way home from the Christmas Sunday School concert. All the children had sung and recited while their parents watched.

Jeremy's class had sung 'O Little Town of Bethlehem' and 'While Shepherds Watched Their Flocks by Night', and his little sister Marian had sung 'Away in a Manger'. Emily was in the oldest Sunday school class and had recited Bible verses telling about the birth of Jesus. After the singing, one of the teachers had told a Christmas story, and each child had received a book from their teacher. And now it was all over, and the family was on its way home.

Jeremy flipped through the pages of his new book. He looked at the bright pictures, not stopping to read the words. Later he would read the story of the shepherds keeping watch over their sheep near Bethlehem. He looked out of the window again. Too bad Christmas was already over. It always took such a long time to come.

'Mom', he called to the front of the car to get her attention. 'Does Christmas always come exactly on December 25?'

'Yes, Jeremy', she replied. 'Why do you ask?'

'That means it's exactly a year away', he answered. 'That's super long. I wish it came every month! That would be the best.'

Jeremy looked out the window again, thinking of how many more months it was until Christmas. Another whole year. He would be in grade four by then! That was a long time to wait.

It would be a whole year until they would sing Christmas carols again. A whole year until they would get a book and candy again. A whole year until they would hear another Christmas story at the program. He especially loved the Christmas story. Mr Parkins had told it this year.

Before he began, Mr Parkins had said that he was going to tell a Christmas story that was not only a very nice story, but also a true story. Something that had really happened. Then he had told about the shepherds – the poorest men and boys of Bethlehem, who spent their nights out on the hillside watching over their sheep.

Jeremy had listened with big eyes as Mr Parkins told about the wolves that would try to get the sheep, how the sheep would wander away, and how robbers could try to steal the sheep.

He could almost feel how cold and dark it was on the hillside. Then 'Suddenly!' Mr Parkins exclaimed, and all the children had jumped in their seats. 'The whole sky lit up, and the shepherds jumped with fright.'

'It was an angel, a holy messenger from God with good news for the shepherds. The angel told them that a Saviour was born: someone to save them from their sins. They could find this baby nearby in the town of Bethlehem. Then the whole sky lit up with many angels singing to God because Jesus was born.

'The shepherds believed the angel's message, and leaving their sheep behind, went to find Jesus. They found Him just like the angel had said, not in a King's palace, but in a stable with animals. And there they worshipped Him. But,' Mr Parkins said, 'the story doesn't end there. When the shepherds left Mary and Joseph and the baby, they started telling everyone about the child, the Saviour that was born. And returning to their sheep, they glorified and praised God.'

The car pulled into the driveway, and Dad turned off the engine. They were home, but Jeremy was still thinking about the story of the shepherds.

'Do you think the shepherds loved the Lord Jesus?' Jeremy asked his Dad as they were getting out of the car.

'I think they loved Him very much', his Dad said, unlocking the front door of the house. 'They believed what the angel told them. Then they went to find and worship Jesus, and then they were so excited, they told everyone else about the Saviour that was born.'

Jeremy pulled off his coat and shoes, then helped Marian unbutton her coat. 'I wish I was a shepherd', he said. 'I could've taken care of some sheep. I would've watched for wolves and robbers and stuff, and then I could have seen the angels and Jesus too.' He sat down on the stairs.

Mom smiled and ruffled Jeremy's hair. 'I bet you would make a good shepherd', she said, hanging up the coats. 'You take good care of Marian. But you don't need to be a shepherd to love Jesus. Jesus is still alive today even though we can't see Him. And we have received the same message that the shepherds did. I know an angel doesn't come to us to tell us about Jesus, but we have the whole Bible telling us about Him!'

Mom began hanging up the coats. 'So what did the shepherds do that we must do?' she asked Jeremy.

'Love the Lord Jesus?' Jeremy asked.

'Yes', Mom replied, 'and what else?'

Jeremy thought for a minute. 'Tell other people about Jesus?'

'That's right!' Mom answered. 'We must believe the message, go and worship the Lord Jesus, and then tell other people about Him.' She reached down and picked up a pair of mittens on the floor. 'Think about how we can do that', she said leaving the hallway.

Jeremy sat still on the bottom step of the stairs for a moment, then followed Mom into the family room. Climbing on to one end of the couch, he settled himself comfortably with his new book and began to read the story of the shepherds. Now he knew that it wasn't just a nice story about some shepherds and angels. It was a story that had really happened. And just as the shepherds had learned that they needed Jesus to save them, this story showed Jeremy that he needed the Saviour too.

8: A JOYFUL NOISE

> *O come, let us sing unto the LORD:*
> *let us make a joyful noise to the rock*
> *of our salvation.*
> Psalm 95:1

Come with me! I'd like to take you on a visit to the Johnsons' house. The Johnsons live in a small brick house on Mulberry Street. There are five children in the family, three girls and two boys, along with their mom and dad.

It's Saturday morning, and Mom is busy vacuuming the house. Dad is outside shovelling the driveway, and Chris is helping him. In the kitchen, Darlene is putting away the break-fast dishes, while Cara practises piano in the living room. Rosa is playing in the family room with little Charles. They have just built a big tower of blocks, and now little Charles is beg-ging Rosa to play 'Ring a Ring o' Roses'[1] with him. Rosa agrees and so they swing around in a circle singing the little song and finally falling to the ground with a big thump. The little boy hops quickly to his feet, 'Do 'gain, Rosa! Do 'gain!' And so

---

[1] The words of this song vary around the world. Use the version you know best!

Rosa climbs back up and starts again, 'Ring a Ring o' Roses, a pocketful of posies . . .'

Everywhere, music is heard. In the living room Cara is slowly, note by note, playing a song. She has finished practising her pieces for this week and is trying to learn a Psalm to surprise her piano teacher. She has chosen Psalm 10, but is having some trouble with the B flat. Still, she keeps practising, and soon she has gone through the whole song twice.

Darlene has nearly finished with the dishes and is humming a song to herself that she has learned at school. Upstairs, Mom sings aloud as she finishes the vacuuming. Outside, Dad whistles a tune as he and Chris tackle the end of the driveway together. It's Saturday, the sun is shining brightly, the family is together, and happiness brings a song to everyone's heart.

Once the chores are finished, Mom calls Dad in for coffee and the children to the kitchen for a snack. Sitting around the table she remarks, 'It's Aunt Carolyn's birthday today, isn't it? We should give her a call for a minute to wish her a happy birthday.' And so Mom dials the phone number and all the children gather around the phone to sing 'Happy Birthday'. Aunt Carolyn laughs when she hears little Charles's voice right in the mouthpiece: 'Happy birsday to woo, happy birsday to woo . . .' But she is glad to hear the children's singing; it makes her day brighter.

Setting down his coffee cup, Dad says, 'You children better get out there and enjoy the snow before it all melts. It's supposed to get warmer in the next few days.' And so the children all hurry to pull on snowpants and boots, mittens, coats, hats, and scarves. So bundled up that he can hardly walk, Charles toddles along behind them as they run laughing out the back door.

Maria, their young neighbour sees them from her backyard and comes over to play. Chris and Darlene are working on a snow fort, and Rosa and Charles are climbing up snow piles and sliding back down. 'Want to go on the swing set with me?' Cara asks Maria. 'We can go really high then go flying off. It won't hurt, because we'll land in the snow!'

'Okay!' Maria says, and the two girls run over to the swings. They begin pushing off with their feet then pulling with their arms, to make the swings go higher and higher. Soon Cara can see over the top of the swing set, and she begins to sing as she flies back and forth, back and forth.

'What are you singing?' Maria laughs as she goes sailing past.

'A song from Sunday school', Cara replies. 'We have to know it for tomorrow. Here I go! Watch out!' she calls and lets herself go flying through the air to land in the snow.

Maria gives a squeal of fright then closes her eyes and follows. Landing with an *oomph* beside Cara, she flops on her back, giggling in the snow.

'Don't you ever just want to sing?' Cara asks Maria. 'Sometimes I just feel so happy inside that I just want to sing. Like . . . everything I have is so good. God takes such good care of me. It just makes me want to sing. Don't you ever have that?' she asks Maria.

'Not really', Maria answers. 'Sometimes I'm happy, but usually it's pretty boring and quiet at my house. Like, my Dad is never there, and my Mom is gone a lot. I go to Grandma's, but there's nothing to do there except watch TV. And even that gets boring after a while. No one seems really happy at my house.'

Maria rolls over on to her stomach to draw figures in the snow. 'Like, no one's mad, or anything, but they don't want to laugh and sing. Even the kids in my class at school don't know how to have fun. All they do is talk about other people and what TV shows they watch at night.'

'That's not much fun', Cara agrees looking at Maria. 'I'm glad my family is usually happy.' She thinks for a minute. 'But you still have lots of the same good things that God gives me. We both have families and friends. And we can play together, like right now. Maybe you can stay over for lunch today; I'll ask my Mom. Do you want to?'

'Yeah! I'll ask my Mom too', Maria agrees. 'She won't care. And it'll be fun to eat over. Are you going to sing from that book again after lunch?' Maria asks. 'You did last time I ate over.'

'Do you mean the Psalter? The blue book?' Cara asks. 'Yeah, we always do. Because we want to sing to God because He gives us everything. Like, He gives us our family, and us to be friends with each other. He even gives us the sun and the snow to play in today!'

Cara climbs up to her feet. 'I guess that's why I was singing on the swing. Because He makes my heart happy, and then I want to sing to Him. Come on', she says pulling Maria to her feet. 'We can learn a Psalm after lunch, and then next time you're happy you can sing too!'

9: TELLING TALES

Lie not against the truth.
James 3:14

Ring! The bell rings for recess to begin, and a flood of children run out of the school on to the playground. A group of children line up for the rings to swing their way across. Trina is ready to go, but suddenly Michelle, an older girl, pushes her to the back of the line.

'I'm first,' Michelle tells Trina.

'But I never got a turn last recess!' Trina protests.

'Yes, you did!' Michelle replies already swinging across. 'You went last!'

'I did not!' Trina denies. 'I was going to have my turn and then the bell rang to come in!'

Who is telling the truth?

Robert, James and Brian climb to the top of the playground equipment. James is telling the other boys about the new snowboard he got for his birthday. Robert listens and wishes that

38

he had a snowboard like that. Brian tells them he has an even better one at home. When Robert asks him why he doesn't take it to school, Brian says he's not allowed to, because he might wreck it.

Robert and James look doubtful. Does Brian really have a better snowboard at home, or is he just trying to sound better than James?

❧

'My crazy carpet[1] is gone! I left it right by the fence, but now it's gone!' Leah and Maria stand at the top of the hill, ready to go down. Leah is upset because she cannot find her crazy carpet. Maria looks around and then says, 'I saw Carol with a red one that looks like yours; she probably took it. She always takes other people's stuff.'

Leah's face becomes angry. 'I'm going to tell on her,' she says. 'She better give it back to me.'

Does Carol always take other people's things, or is Maria being mean?

❧

Out in the soccer field some small children are building a snow fort. Together they roll the snowballs and then carefully place them on the walls. Suddenly a group of older children come racing past, shrieking and laughing. Carelessly they jump over the fort, knocking down one of the walls. One of the little boys runs to tell the teacher, and she calls the students back to find out what happened.

'They broke our fort!' the little children cry.

---

[1] A simple design of children's sled or sledge.

The teacher asks which student broke the wall, but no one answers. Hadn't any of them broken the fort, or were they afraid of getting in trouble?

§&

Have you ever heard this at school? Have you ever argued with your brothers or sisters at home about whose turn it is to go first? Have you ever tried to sound better than someone else? Or tried to make someone else look bad? Have you kept silent so that you would not be punished?

The Lord talks about this behaviour in the ninth commandment: Thou shalt not bear false witness against thy neighbour. This commandment teaches us that we may not lie, exaggerate, or tell bad things about others. We also must not fool people by not saying anything when we are supposed to speak up.

People lie to get their own way. They think about what they want, instead of caring about others. We can see this with Michelle and Trina. Michelle wanted to be first across the rings, so she accused Trina of lying. She was thinking about what she wanted, instead of being fair to Trina. What would you have said if you thought Trina already had her turn last recess?

Some people exaggerate to sound better than others. When James was telling his friends about his birthday present, Brian became jealous. Instead of being happy for James, he wanted to sound just as important. So he told James and Robert that he had a better snowboard at home. What do you say when someone is telling about something they have that you don't have?

You may sometimes hear people saying mean things about others. They want to make someone else sound bad, so that they themselves will look good. And so they tell stories about someone who is not there. Leah's crazy carpet is missing, and Maria immediately accuses Carol of taking it. She says that Carol always takes things, making Carol sound bad. What do you do when people say something mean about someone else? Do you laugh and tell some more things about them, or do you defend them?

Sometimes people do not say anything when they are afraid of getting in trouble. They will not admit that they have done something wrong. When those older students broke the small children's snow fort, no one admitted it to the teacher because they were afraid of getting into trouble. Now the small children are angry with them, the teacher cannot trust them to tell the truth, and they have a guilty conscience before God. How do you answer when you are asked about something you have done wrong?

🐌

We all have broken the ninth commandment. Every one of us has lied, or exaggerated, or said untrue things about others. The Lord takes lying seriously. You may know the story of Ananias and Sapphira. Ananias and Sapphira were a man and woman who lied to the apostles. They sold a piece of land and gave some of the money to the church. That was nice of them. But then they told Peter that they had given all of the money to the church. First Ananias came and lied to Peter, and immediately God struck him down dead. Soon Sapphira came, and she lied too. God also struck her down dead. We can read in Zechariah 8:17 that God hates lying. And He tells us in Proverbs 19:5 that 'he that speaketh lies shall not escape'. God will punish liars.

41

Is there no hope then? Or is there a way to be forgiven? Turn for a moment to Proverbs 28:13. There we read, 'He that covereth his sins shall not prosper: but whoso confesseth and forsaketh them shall have mercy.' If we pretend we have not sinned, or try to hide our sin from our parents, and teachers, and God, we will get into more trouble. But if we confess that we have sinned and repent from doing so any more, then God will forgive us our sins. ✌

10: PAINTED EGGS

> *Jesus said unto her, 'I am the resurrection, and the life.'*
> John 11:25a

Ding-dong!

'I'll go!' Mikayla exclaimed. She dropped the red marker she was holding and jumped to her feet. Pausing by the window, she peeked out to see who was standing on the front porch. It was a neighbour and her little sister.

Mikayla smiled and swung open the door. 'Hi, Susannah! Did you want to come over and play in the backyard?'

'Not today', Susannah said. 'Here.' She gave Mikayla a pink paper and smiled at her. 'The town is having an Easter egg hunt. All the kids are invited.'

'Oh boy!' Mikayla said and waved as Susannah and her sister set off to deliver more fliers.

Mikayla turned and ran to the kitchen where Dad was repairing the kitchen sink. 'Dad! Guess what?' she called to the legs and feet sticking out from the cupboard. 'Me and Alaina are invited to an Easter egg hunt! See? I got an invitation!'

Dad twisted sideways to peer out of the cupboard. 'Was that Susannah at the door?' he asked. When Mikayla nodded, he continued. 'Listen. I know it sounds fun, but you can't go. If you check the invitation, it probably is going to be held tomorrow, on Easter Sunday.'

Mikayla's face fell as she checked the invitation. Dad was right. But she had wanted so badly to go.

'Besides', Dad went on as he twisted a wrench around the pipe, 'Easter eggs is not what Easter is about. Easter is when we remember the Lord Jesus rising from the dead.'

'Then why do people hide Easter eggs?' Mikayla asked.

'Well', Dad grunted as he tightened a washer, 'Eggs have had special meaning to people for hundreds of years. People in countries like Egypt, Africa, China, and even ancient Gaul, Persia and Phoenicia used eggs as a part of their worship. They believed that their gods brought new life to the earth every spring, and they used an egg as a symbol of this new life. The eggs were held in reverence and believed to have special powers. People carried them with them or buried them under their buildings to chase away evil. Later on people began painting the eggs or wrapping them in gold and exchanging them.'

'But we don't worship eggs or believe that they have special power', Mikayla said.

Dad poked his head out of the cupboard again. 'I know, Mikayla. But the biggest problem when we get involved with Easter eggs and Easter bunnies, is that we forget what Easter really is about. And that's what Satan loves. He would rather we had our mind filled with eggs and bunnies than with the Lord Jesus. Doesn't he do the same thing at Christmas?' Dad asked.

'Satan would rather have us think about Santa Claus than about the Lord Jesus' birth.'

Mikayla listened quietly. She looked once more at the invitation and with a sigh, dropped it into the recycling bin.

Just then Mom came down the stairs. 'I have to run over to the grocery store to pick up a few things', she said to the feet sticking out of the cupboard. 'I'll take the girls with me. Mikayla, can you call Alaina?'

A few minutes later they were driving off in the van. 'Look!' Alaina exclaimed as they pulled onto Main Street. A long purple banner was hanging over the bookstore. 'What does it say?' she asked.

Mikayla read the sign out loud. 'Join us Sunday for Easter Egg Painting.'

'Oh! Can we go?' Alaina asked excitedly.

'Not on Sunday, silly', Mikayla said, and she thought with disappointment about the Easter egg hunt.

In the grocery store, the girls helped Mom get the things on her list. Soon they were ready to pay. Over by the check-outs, a small area was blocked off by ropes. A big purple chair sat in the middle, and balloons floated in the air all around it.

'What's that for?' Alaina asked as Mom unloaded the cart.

Again Mikayla read the sign. 'Come get your picture taken with the Easter bunny, Sunday 9:00 – 12:00.'

'What's an Easter bunny?' Alaina asked.

'It's a person dressed up in a costume like a big rabbit', Mikayla said.

'But why do they dress up like a rabbit?' Alaina persisted.

Mikayla thought for a moment, then shrugged. 'I don't know why; they just do.'

As they pulled out the parking lot, Mikayla asked Mom about the Easter bunny.

'The Easter bunny?' Mom repeated as she checked both ways for cars. 'I think that's been around for many years. It really has nothing to do with Easter as we celebrate it in church. Instead, many years ago, people in different countries worshipped the Eostre goddess. You see, instead of worshipping the true God, they made up their own gods and goddesses and worshipped them. They believed that each of their gods had different powers. For example, the sun god had the power to give light and heat and was represented by a picture of the sun.

'They named one of their goddesses Eostre, and they believed that she had the power to make new life and to make things grow. Each spring they had a pagan festival to worship their goddess. The picture that they used to represent her was the rabbit, and so the rabbit soon became known in the festival as the Eostre rabbit.

'The Germans first brought this symbol to North America over a hundred years ago. And from the Eostre rabbit, we now have the name Easter bunny.'

'So that's why we don't take pictures with the Easter bunny?' Alaina asked Mom. 'Because we don't want to worship the Easter lady and the Easter rabbit?'

'That's right', Mom said as she steered the van into the driveway.

❦

'Hey look!' Alaina called from the window the next morning. It was Sunday, and the girls were getting ready for church.

'There goes Susannah and her brother and Emily', she told Mikayla.

Mikayla hurried to the window to look. Sure enough, Susannah was walking by with her brother and sister. Both girls were swinging small baskets. 'They're going to the Easter egg hunt in the park', Mikayla said. With a sigh she turned away from the window and pulled on her shoes for church.

At church, everyone seemed to be smiling. The girls waited patiently as Mom and Dad shook hands with the other adults. 'Blessed Easter', they heard them say. 'Blessed Easter.'

At last it was time for Sunday school. Mikayla sat down next to one of her friends and waited for the teacher to start her lesson.

'Today we have a special lesson on Easter', the teacher began. 'Easter brings good news to us and to all the world who will hear. Do you know what this good news is?'

Mikayla's friend raised her hand. 'It's about how the Lord Jesus didn't stay dead. About how He is still alive today in heaven and can also live in our hearts.'

'That's right', the teacher said. 'At this time of year it seems like the whole world is talking about Easter. Driving to church I could see signs for Easter egg hunts and Easter sales and Easter bunnies. Everyone is busy trying to find something to fill their hearts that will make them happy. But there is no truth in these events, and there is nothing lasting in them.

'The real message of Easter was not written on a purple banner, but was given by the angels at the Lord Jesus' grave: 'He is not here, but is risen.' This is what happened on the resurrection morning . . .'

Mikayla and Alaina were dressing their dolls on the deck as Mom and Dad had coffee. Suddenly the girls heard the neighbour's screen door open and bang shut. They looked up and saw Susannah coming out the house with a basket of Easter eggs. For a moment, Mikayla felt the disappointment and envy come back into her heart, but then she watched, surprised, as Susannah's brother called her from the porch. Susannah ran back to the house, her basket bouncing beside her.

Alaina exclaimed as she saw the chocolate eggs bounce out of the basket into the grass, but Susannah didn't even stop or seem to care. She was arguing loudly with her brother about why he gets to go bowling with his friends, and not her. Just before she reached the door, he slammed it shut in her face.

'Mom!' Susannah shouted out in anger and rushed into the house. Slam! The door closed again and quiet filled the back yard once more.

'I guess Easter eggs don't make you happy', Mikayla said slowly, staring at the colourful eggs lying in Susannah's yard.

Alaina nodded her head. 'Only Jesus makes you happy', she piped up.

What are you trying to fill your heart with? What will bring you lasting happiness?

11: IN MY HEART

> *Let brotherly love continue.*
> Hebrews 13:1

Tweet! Tweet! The tiny bird hopped across the window-sill, tilting his black-capped head from side to side. *Tweet! Tweet!* Through the glass he could see a girl lying on the family room floor, slowly turning the pages of a new Christmas catalogue, and circling toys with a bright pink marker.

'Melanie!' the girl's mom called. 'Are you learning your verses for Sunday School?'

'Sort of', the girl answered pushing herself up off the ground and picking up the index card that she had been using as a bookmark. With one last look at the book-marked doll – a beautiful doll with eyes that opened and closed, and silky hair to comb – she closed the catalogue. 'Remember the words of the Lord Jesus,' she recited as she walked down the hall to her bedroom. 'How he said, "It is more blessed to give than to receive." "Freely ye have received, freely give." *Acts* 20:35 and *Matthew* 10:8.'

Hop! Hop! The little bird left a trail of tiny footprints on the snow-dusted window-sill, then with a flash of his wings, darted through the air to the bedroom window-sill nearby. Fluttering down to the ledge he watched as Melanie picked up the doll on her bed and running a brush through her tangled hair, set it back down with a sigh.

Chirrup! Tweet! Tweet! the chickadee chirped. And he cocked his head to one side. Spying the bird on the windowsill, Melanie dropped the doll to the bed and went to get her coat. 'Mom,' she called. 'Can I go play outside for a while before it gets too dark?'

〄

The sky was growing dark and snow was beginning to fall as the chickadee left his perch in the evergreen tree. Melanie was rolling a snowman in the front yard, but both she and bird paused and watched as a woman and her daughter trudged home from the bus stop. Their coats and shoes were well-worn and looked as tired and cheerless as their faces. *Chirrup!* the little bird called as they turned in a driveway, and he fluttered down to land on the mailbox below. 27 Prescott Road, announced the faded red letters.

For a moment the girl's face brightened at the sight of the cheery little bird, but her mother tugged her arm and she followed, up the cracked steps and into the dark house for a supper of bread and cheap noodles.

The snow fell harder and the little bird fluffed his feathers before flying off. He would make one more visit to the bird-feeder before night came.

〄

'Oh, there you are, Melanie,' Mom said as she looked in her bedroom door. 'Are you still studying your text for Sunday School? I thought you would know it off by heart by now.' And Mom glanced at the new doll slipped neatly back into the box that it had come in. Oh, she could still see Melanie's bright eyes last night, as she pulled out the doll and smoothed back her silky hair.

Melanie was getting her New Testament from her bedside table as Mom leaned forward for a better look at the doll. What was that note tied on a ribbon around her neck?

To the girl at
27 Prescott Road.

'Melanie?' Mom asked questioningly.

And Melanie came over and slipped the small Bible also into the doll's box. 'Oh, I do know my text by heart now, Mom. I even know it in my heart.'

ᦥ

Tweet! Tweet! the chickadee called from the telephone wire above. He cocked his head as Melanie pulled open the squeaky mailbox door and thrust the long box inside. The door wouldn't close, but with a quick good-bye to her doll, she hurried home. The sky was growing grey with the promise of more snow, but Melanie's heart was light.

With a flutter of wings, the bird landed on the windowsill of the cheerless home. *Chirrup! Chirrup!* he called loudly, and a pale oval face appeared in the window. Hopping back and forth, the little bird waited until the girl came to the door. Then he fluttered to the mailbox. *Tweet! Tweet!* he called. And the girl came. Reaching to close the mailbox door, she saw the end of the box poking out. It was as though the sun came out, so bright was the light in her eyes when she saw the note. 'Look, Mom!' she called, running eagerly up the cracked porch steps. 'A doll and a book for me!'

Twitter! Twitter! Tweet! the bird called, and he flew off to find a roost for the night.

12: PRAYER IN THE PALACE

> *This poor man cried, and the Lord heard him, and saved him out of all his troubles.*
> Psalm 34:6

In a far-away country, in the capital city, stands a palace. Surrounded by high walls and heavy gates, the palace is safe from all enemies. Gardens and orchards can be seen surrounding the palace, and the gates leading to the palace doors stand wide open. Come, let us enter this gate.

One of the king's messengers stands before us, and following him up a wide walkway to the palace steps, we enter through the massive doors. Here we find ourselves in a great hall. The hall is bright and beautiful, with marble pillars and tiled floors. Richly embroidered tapestries hang on the walls between tall narrow windows.

At the far end of the hall, wide steps lead up to a throne, and there a king sits, a golden sceptre in his hand. We watch as messengers hurry to and from the king, bowing deeply before him. Bringing the king news, and taking his orders, they hurry to carry out his commands. As we listen, royal decrees are proclaimed, soldiers are sent to battle, the guilty are judged, and the innocent are set free.

On the right hand of the king we can see another throne, and on it sits the crown prince. We watch again as a messenger comes before the king. The crown prince listens to his request also, and then leans toward the king to speak with him. The king grants the messenger his request, and he hurries away to obey the king's orders. And so it goes on all morning long, as a steady stream of people enter and leave the royal palace.

At last we step back out into the bright sunshine and, following our guide, walk back to the open gates. There our attention is caught by a small boy standing outside the gate. With his hands wrapped tightly around the rungs of the gate, he is looking up at the great white palace. From his appearance, he seems to be a beggar. His hands and face are dirty, his feet are bare, and his clothes are ragged. Yet on his face is a look of hope.

Our guide stops and asks the boy what he is doing here, but at first the young boy is too frightened to answer.

'Speak up, child,' the messenger says kindly. 'Why have you come, and to whom do you need to speak?'

The boy stares at the ground for a moment, and then finally answers. 'I need to speak to the king,' he says hesitantly.

'Truly?' the messenger asks. 'Who sent you?'

'I am in great trouble,' the boy replies. 'I have no father and mother, and no friends to care for me. There is no one to help me, and so I need to speak to the king.'

'And how did you find your way here?' the messenger asks the small boy.

'There was a man who knew of my troubles,' the boy tells him, 'and although he could not help me, he said there was someone who could. He told me to follow the road leaving my village and that when I reached its end, I would find a great and kind king, and he would help me. And so I have walked a long way, and I cannot wait any longer.'

The boy's face is becoming frightened. May he not speak to the king after all? Perhaps he is too small, or unimportant? Too ragged and too dirty?

'I need to speak to the king,' the boy repeats urgently.

'Then, come in,' the messenger invites him, and a smile lights up the boy's face. 'For all are welcome here. The king turns no one away, and the prince will hear every request.'

We turn and watch as the little ragged boy goes hand in hand up the walkway with our guide. Entering the palace hall, he comes before the king to tell him of his troubles.

We also have a great and kind King in heaven. He is willing to hear all our troubles. Do you go often to Him in prayer?

13: CURLS AND SPLINTERS

> *Whose adorning . . . let it be the hidden man of*
> *the heart . . . even the ornament of a meek and quiet*
> *spirit, which is in the sight of God of great price.*
> 1 Peter 3:3–4

Running barefoot across the cool barn floor, Jolene looked back to see if her cousin was coming. Envy filled her eyes as Keisha flipped a long golden curl back over her shoulder. Her own hair was neither blonde nor brown, and, oh, so poker straight. With a frown, Jolene looked down at her own worn clothes, comfortably faded and perfect for farm-living. No, Keisha was obviously the city girl in her suede sandals with the white flower by the toes, and her pleated skirt with a matching top.

But still, it was not Keisha's clothes that caused a flame of envy to burn hot in Jolene's breast; for the clothes would get dirty and worn, and why, someday when Jolene was older and could get a job, she would save up her money and buy clothes just as nice as Keisha's. No, it was the golden curls that made Jolene frown. Try as she might to brush some shine into her own hair, even coaxing her older sister into curling it Sunday morning before church, it never looked like Keisha's. For even the stiff curls could not hide the drab plainness of her mouse-coloured hair. And by the time Sunday School was out, so were Jolene's curls, hanging limply down her back.

'Hurry up, Keisha!' Jolene called back as she climbed the worn wooden ladder to the hayloft above. There the two girls clambered up some straw bales before arranging them to make a fort. Jolene had the best ideas and designed a tunnel leading to a secret doorway while Keisha eagerly helped. Then, tiring of their finished fort, the girls scrambled to the highest hay pile they could find to play king-of-the-hill. The prickly straw didn't seem to bother Jolene as she scurried nimbly to the top of the slippery pile and pushed Keisha back down. How she laughed as over and over Keisha slid back down, not once making it to the top. But pride goeth before . . . a fall, and in a moment of glee, Jolene stepped back a little too far, and catching her foot in the twine of a straw bale, went tumbling down, head over heels.

Quick as a wink, Keisha climbed to the top; she was king of the hill! Now it was her turn to laugh good-naturedly as Jolene got up and dusted herself off, but Jolene did not join in the laughter. Oh, she could laugh when Keisha tumbled down, but to be the one laughed at? That was not something that Jolene could take. Not even a smile tugged at her lips as she pressed them together in determination and scrambled furiously to where Keisha perched at the top.

Sunlight streamed through a crack in the barn walls outlining Keisha's curls in a bright gold as she covered her mouth and giggled.

The flame of envy burned brighter in Jolene's breast. 'I'm going to get you!' she said angrily, and hoisting herself up the last two bales, she pitched wildly forward and snatched at Keisha's ponytail.

'Don't!' Keisha cried as she lost her balance. Stumbling to gain hers, Jolene also wobbled, and suddenly they both went down as the whole straw pile eased over and with a great thumping and bumping came tumbling down.

'Ouch!' Jolene cried out, for as she reached out to the wall to stop her fall, a sharp splinter of wood pierced the palm of her hand. Pulling her hand free, she looked over at Keisha.

'Oooooh. Ow,' Keisha groaned as she pulled herself up. Then her eyes turned to the disastrous pile of hay bales. 'Look what you did, Jolene,' she said with raised eyebrows. 'Your dad's going to be mad.' But Jolene didn't seem to hear her, for she was busy inspecting her hand.

'What happened?' Keisha asked while leaning in for a better look. 'Did you get a splinter? Ouch! You better get your mom to pull that out right away before it goes in deeper.'

Jolene, who had been holding the painful hand close to her face, suddenly let it drop. 'No!' she announced putting on a tough farm-girl attitude. 'It will be fine. I'm not a *baby*, you know.'

Keisha shrugged and turned to follow Jolene down out of the hayloft.

'Let's bike out to the back pasture,' Jolene said, but soon wished she hadn't, for as she gripped the handlebars, the splinter seemed to slide in deeper and bothered her more and more. Stopping by the back fence, Keisha called to the cows who just kept on grazing. Jolene had been peering at her hand, but when Keisha hopped back on her bike, Jolene's eyes were again caught by the sight of her cousin's golden curls. Even the sight of rough straw clinging to Keisha's ponytail could not ease her envy.

Arriving at the back pasture, the girls dropped their bikes by the pond. Collecting fallen pieces of bark, they floated them in the water, adding acorns for sailors and fashioning sails out of leaves. Normally Jolene would have been pleased with the way her boat caught the breeze and floated along the water's edge, while Keisha's kept flipping upside down. But, instead, Jolene inspected the splinter in her hand. Oh, did it ever hurt! Stupid thing, she thought, for it was starting to throb.

Keisha noticed Jolene's pain and came over to where she stood. 'Let me see it,' she asked reaching for Jolene's hand.

'No, it's fine,' Jolene said pressing her thumb tightly against it, shoving the splinter in deeper. Then, abruptly, she turned. 'Let's go home,' she said.

୫

Poking around in her mom's sewing drawer, Jolene looked for a needle to help get out the splinter. Instead, her eyes lit on her mom's sharp sewing shears, the special scissors that were kept sharp for cutting fabric.

'I have an idea,' Jolene said suddenly, forgetting about the splinter for a moment. 'Let's play hair-dresser.'

Keisha turned to her with interest. 'Okay!' she said.

'I'll be the hairdresser first,' Jolene said quickly. 'You sit here,' she ordered and shoved the sewing chair behind Keisha.

Obediently Keisha sat, and with a wild gleam in her eyes, Jolene grasped Keisha's ponytail with one hand and snatched the scissors out of the drawer with the other. One big satisfying *SNIP!* and Keisha's curls lay in a golden heap on the floor.

Jolene's triumphant smile faded at Keisha's horrified gasp, and the two girls stared for a moment at the pony-tail lying on the floor. Dropping the scissors to the floor, Jolene turned and fled.

&

'It's going to hurt,' Dad said as he pressed the needle and tweezers against the skin of Jolene's hand.

Tears filled Jolene's eyes, but she squeezed her mouth and eyes tightly shut. There had been enough tears that afternoon. Tears from Keisha, and tears from her. Tears of anger and tears of repentance. She still wasn't sure if Keisha had forgiven her. After all, how could Keisha? Jolene certainly would not have spoken to Keisha again if Keisha had done the same to her.

Mom was away right now, driving Keisha home. She hadn't wanted to stay the night any more. So now Dad was trying to get out the bothersome splinter. The skin on Jolene's hand was an angry red and had grown swollen around the spot where the splinter had pierced the skin.

'Boy, you sure managed to get this in deep,' Dad murmured as he pressed hard against her hand with the tweezers. With a final burning pain, he pinched, then, 'A-ha!' he said as he pulled out the long thin piece of wood.

Laying the instruments on the table, Dad sat back with a sigh and looked at Jolene.

'Why *did* you cut Keisha's hair?' he finally asked.

For a moment Jolene just stared at him, and then her chin trembled and the whole story came sobbing out: how her hair was so poker straight and Keisha always looked so pretty, and no matter how she tried to curl her hair it never looked nice and, oh, how she wished she could have golden hair too, or at least curls and, oh, how ugly she was.

By this time Jolene was on Dad's lap and crying against his shoulder.

'Jolene,' Dad said, lifting her face. 'Look at me. The only thing that is ugly about you, is the character that you have shown today. Envy is an ugly thing that starts festering as it grows deeper and stronger inside you.'

'Just like my splinter went deeper and hurt more?' Jolene asked lifting up her sore hand so that she could see the bandage.

'Exactly,' Dad said. 'That splinter should have been pulled out the moment it went in, and you need to do the same with envy. When an envious thought comes into your mind, push it out. Don't think about it for one more moment.'

Jolene was watching Dad's face as he spoke. 'That's hard to do,' she said, 'but, I know, you are going to tell me to ask the Lord to help me.'

Dad smiled. 'You're right again. He will pull out those seeds of envy every time they are planted, if you ask.'

Jolene slid off Dad's knee. Already her hand was starting to feel a little better. But she still had one more worry. 'Do you think Keisha will ever forgive me?' she asked.

'Well,' Dad said. 'Soon the skin will grow again on your hand and your hand will heal. You can heal your relationship too with Keisha by confessing your sin and asking her forgiveness.'

'I already did,' Jolene told him.

'That's good,' Dad said, 'but you have to give her time. Your hand won't heal in a day, and neither will your friendship. Keisha may need time to see that you're truly sorry. In the meantime, you must pray and work at keeping your heart clean from sin. Then you will have a beauty that shines out from the inside: not the beauty of golden curls, but the joy and love that spills from a new heart and puts a sparkle in your eye and a happy expression on your face.' ❧

14: THE FISHING SHOW

> *For where your treasure is,*
> *there will your heart be also.*
> Matthew 6:21

Beep, beep, beep, went Carl's alarm clock, and his eyes popped open. In an instant, he had jumped out of bed and thrown open the curtains. A stream of sunlight caught him right in the eyes. 'Yes! Perfect weather for the fishing show,' he exclaimed.

His older brother Rob was already downstairs. Carl joined him for a quick breakfast, then hurried out to the truck. He was almost as excited about riding in Rob's shiny new pickup, as he was about going to the fishing show. He didn't often get to go places with his older brother, because Rob usually had to work on Saturdays. When he had free time, he would rather spend it with his cousin Pete than with his little brother.

'Have a good time!' Mom called after them. 'And don't get lost,' she added to Carl.

Soon they were off cruising down the highway in the big F150. For a moment Carl expected Rob to crank up the radio; he had always played his music very loudly in his old car. But then he remembered that that had all changed a few weeks ago.

Carl could clearly remember that Saturday when Rob was cleaning his car before selling it. He had asked if he could help. Instead of telling him to 'get lost' as he usually did, Rob had stopped vacuuming, looked at him for a second, and then said, 'Sure.' Together they had washed, waxed, and shined it until they could see their reflections. But when Carl had stacked up all the loose CDs in the car, Rob had picked them up and thrown them with the rest of the garbage. Carl had been shocked. He knew that a single CD could easily cost twenty dollars.

'Why are you throwing out all those CDs?' he finally dared to ask.

'They're garbage,' Rob said, and Carl knew that he meant the music on them.

Finished, they had put a *FOR SALE* sign in the gleaming windshield.

And so, today there was no loud music, only gladness in Carl's heart when he saw how his brother had changed. He couldn't help thinking that when he grew up, he wanted to be just like Rob.

The show was in Toronto, and it took over an hour to get there. After paying admission, Carl followed his brother over to the fishing tackle booths. A dazzling array of bright colours and shiny metals glinted in the sun. Within moments the salesman had pulled out a few of the latest lures. Both Rob and Carl listened intently as the salesman explained what kind of fish each lure was for, and the special features that made it a winner.

Moving along, the boys stopped at a fishing rod display. Rob was fascinated by the sleek new rod and reel combos. Carl admired the smooth rods and shiny reels. He felt the cushioned grips and pretended he had a big one on his line. The salesman came over to Rob to point out the different features of the rods, and Carl listened carefully as he compared 6-foot and 7-foot rods and their different sensitivities. He also demonstrated the spinning versus bait-casting reels. Carl was learning all he could.

After spending some time in the rod and tackle area, the boys headed over to the fishing boats on display. They stopped to admire a Lund and listened in as the salesman gave a talk. Carl was a little lost when he started talking about the different kinds of fish finders, but he did spy the swivel seats the salesman was demonstrating, as well as the down-riggers.

When the salesman had finished his talk, Rob went over to ask a few questions. The two got into a discussion on inboard versus outboard motors and horse-power. Carl didn't understand the half of it, but he was proud to be included in the discussion and tried to remember all he heard.

As they walked away, Carl's stomach growled, reminding him of his early breakfast and coming lunch. It was still early, but Rob bought them both a hotdog from a nearby stand.

They spent the next hour finishing their tour of the fishing show, and then went back to look at two of their favourite exhibits. It was two o'clock by now, and Carl was beginning to get tired from all the excitement and walking. He was glad when Rob said it was about time they were leaving. Clutching a handful of fishing brochures and boat pamphlets, Carl climbed gladly into the truck and sank down into the comfortable seats.

He gave a happy sigh. Rob slid the gear into reverse and grinned at him.

'Have fun?' he asked.

'Yeah, that was awesome,' Carl answered.

'Well, we got some new ideas for bass lures, anyways,' Rob said revving the engine. 'Can't wait to get out on the water next week.'

'Yeah, I just wish it wasn't Sunday tomorrow. Then we could go fishing tomorrow,' Carl said eagerly.

'Yeah, buddy?' Rob backed the truck out of its parking spot. 'Fishing isn't everything, you know. It's great fun, but it's not what matters in the end. Going to church is a whole lot more important than going fishing.'

Carl thought about that for a minute. 'I guess so,' he agreed reluctantly. 'I mean, I know it's more important, but it doesn't seem fun,' he added.

Rob smiled. 'Church isn't meant to be fun, you know that,' he said. 'But what I mean is that what you learn at church is for your soul. Sure, fishing is fun for the outside of you, but the sermon is a message for the inside of you. It warns you about the bad ways that you can go, and encourages you about the good way of serving God.'

Carl looked at his brother doubtfully. 'You never used to think that,' he said bluntly.

'I know,' Rob said. 'And I was very wrong. God showed me how wasteful I was being with my life. And how sinful. He's the One that changed me.' Rob shoulder-checked then pulled out on to the highway. 'And that's what made the difference for me in church. Now it's not boring anymore, but gives me all the help I need for the next week.'

'But it can still be pretty hard to understand, for me,' Carl said. 'Sometimes I don't even know what the minister is talking about,' he added honestly.

'I know,' Rob said. 'But you can give it your best attention – just like at the fishing show today. I'm sure you didn't get everything, but your attention was still glued because you wanted to understand, right?'

Carl nodded.

'And I guess that's what makes the difference in church too,' Rob continued thoughtfully. 'It's so much easier to listen and learn if you want to be there and you want to understand.'

Carl watched the cars go by. He thought about what Rob had said. Was that really it? Was it so much easier to listen and learn at the fishing show because he *wanted* to be there? Sure, some parts of the sermon in church were difficult for him to understand, but was the real problem with his *heart*? That he didn't even *want* to listen and learn?

What do you think?

15: THE BEST DAY OF ALL

Kerry bounced out of bed and pulled up the window blind. The sun was rising above the trees, turning icicles into spears of light and the yard into a dazzling spread of snow. Humming a song to herself, she turned to yank the covers up over her pillow and quickly got dressed. In her excitement she zipped the ribbon from her dress up into the zipper. But she couldn't slow down. Not today! It was her birthday! Singing aloud, she pulled a brush through her hair, then dashed down the stairs.

'Hi Dad!' she called to her dad who was getting breakfast ready. 'What are we having for breakfast?'

'Good morning, Kerry,' Dad answered. 'I wonder why you're so happy. Let's see . . . it must be because we're having your favourite breakfast – waffles!'

'No, Dad! It's my birthday! I'm eleven today! How could you forget?' And Kerry ran over to give him a hug.

'Just teasing,' said Dad, rumpling her hair. 'Happy birthday! Now set the table for breakfast, please, then help Mom get Charles and Taylor ready for church. She has her hands full with Kristin and the baby.'

'Awww, can't Charles and Taylor get ready themselves?' Kerry complained. 'And why do I always have to set the table? It's my birthday today!'

'Kerry,' Dad turned to look at her. 'Do as I asked you without complaining.'

Kerry turned and began setting the table in a careless way so that the cups did not match up with the plates, and the knives and forks lay helter-skelter across the table. Finished, she walked into the family room and picked up a book she was reading. Flipping it open to the bookmark, she began to read.

'Kerry,' Mom called from the stairs. 'Could you come up and help Charles and Taylor get ready for church?'

Kerry sighed noisily and trudged upstairs, banging the book against the railing at every step. 'How come I always have to do everything?' she muttered to herself. 'It's my birthday; I should get to do nothing today. And it's Sunday today, so I can't even have a birthday party today. It's not fair.'

With every step she felt more and more sorry for herself. By the time she reached her brothers' room, Kerry was scowling. Quickly she helped them wash their faces, wet and comb their hair, and get dressed, all without saying one word. She ignored Charles when he asked her why she was acting so mean, and she stuck out her tongue at Taylor when he said maybe birthdays made people mean.

Breakfast went even worse. Mom wished Kerry a happy birthday, but Kerry would not even look up as she said thanks.

69

Mom looked at Dad to see what was the matter, but Dad just shrugged. Kerry had two waffles, but she found them hard to swallow. Mom and Dad were quieter than usual, and Charles and Taylor weren't laughing and teasing each other like they usually did.

Kerry wished she hadn't been so mean to them this morning. It wasn't their fault she was feeling so grumpy. She tried to think of something nice to say, to make everyone stop being so quiet.

Just then Charles reached for the jug of orange juice, but it was too heavy for him, and it slipped out of his hand. Orange juice poured all over the table and on to Kerry's lap.

'Charles!' Kerry exclaimed jumping to her feet. She forgot all about saying something nice. 'Look what you did! Now I'm soaking wet!'

'A flood!' said little Kristin clapping her hands. 'It's a flood!'

'Hush, Kristin,' Mom said grabbing a dishtowel. Dad went to get a wet rag to mop the floor, and Mom began drying off the table.

'Run upstairs and change,' she told Kerry. 'You can wear your blue dress; it's just as nice as this one, and I ironed it yesterday.'

'But I wanted to wear this one,' Kerry protested with tears in her eyes. 'Why did Charles dump the juice all over me? Why does everything have to go wrong? How come everything bad happens to me?' she cried, and she turned and ran up the stairs to her room.

Once again everyone was quiet around the breakfast table.

'Kerry,' Mom called out a few minutes later as she pushed open the door to her bedroom. Coming in, she sat on the bed next to her and put her arm around her.

'You're not having a very good day, are you?' Mom asked. When Kerry shook her head no, Mom went on. 'You thought it would be a happy day because it's your birthday, but it hasn't turned out that way. Why do you think that is?'

'I don't know,' Kerry sniffed. 'I was being mean to Charles and to Taylor, and I didn't listen to Dad to help you this morning, and then the juice spilt all on me, and I can't have a birthday party today, and it's not a nice birthday at all!'

Dad came to the door with Kristin in his arms and Taylor in tow. Mom looked up, then turned again to Kerry. 'It's special to be able to share your birthday with the Lord's Day. You see, Sunday is a day to talk and read and hear about the good things God has done. And one of the really special things He has done in our family is He gave us you!'

Dad stepped into the room and set Kristin down. 'I still remember how tiny you were when you were born, Kerry. And how excited we were to take you home from the hospital and put you in your own little bed. See, you are one of the good things God gave us . . . something good for us to remember on His Day.'

Taylor bounced up on the bed next to Mom, and Charles came in holding one shoe. 'What else can you think of that God has done for us?' Dad asked the boys.

They thought for a moment, then Charles piped up, 'He made baby Kristin.'

'And the ark!' Taylor added. 'And in Sunday school we heard about the Good Samaritan. God made him good.'

'And what's the best thing God gave?' Mom asked.

'The Bible?' Charles said. 'A church?'

'No,' Mom answered, 'something even better. It's the reason

71

why we are allowed to pray to God even. Maybe you can help, Kerry.'

Kerry looked up. 'He gave the Lord Jesus.'

'Yes, that was a big thing for God to give,' Dad said and sat down on the bed with the others. 'God gave His own Son. That is the biggest sacrifice that was ever made. It should not be so hard then for all of you to give help to Mom and Dad and each other. When you love and obey God, you will learn to love and obey in your family.'

Kerry thought about how she had wanted everything to go her way. She hadn't thought about how special the Lord's Day was, and why God had made Sunday.

'Loving and obeying God are the things that make you happy,' Dad added, 'not birthdays and less work. When you learn about the good things that God has done for you, then you are glad to do nice things for others. Then Sunday is a special day to learn more and more about God, so we can serve Him better and better.'

16: SANDBOX TEMPTATIONS

> *Greater is he that is in you,*
> *than he that is in the world.*
> 1 John 4:4

It was a beautiful spring day, and the children were playing outside in just their shorts and tee-shirts. The sun was shining brightly, and the puddles from yesterday's rain shower were already dry.

Ryan, Anita, and Linda had been having races up and down the long driveway on their bikes. Linda always got a big head-start because she still rode a tricycle. How her little legs pumped to try to keep up with the others as they flew by! Ryan had already won three races and Anita had won one.

Soon the children grew tired from all that racing, and were feeling hot and sweaty.

'I know!' Anita said suddenly as they pedalled back to the house. 'Let's go build a town in the sandbox. The sand might still be a little wet from yesterday; it'll be perfect for building with!'

'All right,' Ryan agreed.

'I'm gonna help too!' Linda called and came bumping along behind them, pedals spinning.

A town began taking shape in the big square sandbox as each child took a separate corner to work on. Ryan was building a mountain with a tunnel through it, while Anita was making a farm. Linda was building a tower. 'It'll be the CN tower,'[1] she told her brother and sister. They looked at the small bump of sand and hid their smiles.

When Anita's farm was almost finished, she sat back on the edge of the sandbox to see what else she could add. 'I know!' she exclaimed suddenly. 'I need a little pond in the pasture.'

'You better not,' Ryan warned her. 'Mom didn't like it last year when we flooded the sandbox and got our clothes filthy.'

'Oh, I'm not going to make it all mucky,' Anita answered. 'I'm just going to make a little pond. What's so bad about that?' And with that, she hopped up and ran off. A minute later she returned with the garden hose. Carefully she turned on the water and filled the hollow she had carved out.

'There,' she said with satisfaction. 'Now the animals can drink.'

Ryan looked from Anita's farm to his mountain. 'What I need is a mountain stream running through this tunnel,' he said. 'Pass me the hose, will you?' Anita looked surprised but passed him the hose. Soon Ryan had a small river running through his mountain.

Anita came over to inspect his work. 'That looks cool,' she agreed, "but you should add a waterfall; that would be awesome.'

[1] Until recently, the tallest tower in the world.

After Ryan added his waterfall, Linda helped herself to the garden hose. 'I need a moat around my castle,' she informed Anita. 'The tower wasn't going so good, so I made it into a castle instead.'

Anita watched doubtfully as Linda filled her moat with water, but then Ryan came over and exclaimed, 'Hey! I know. We should combine our streams so that the water can run from here to the waterfall, to your pond, then back to Linda's moat.'

And so it went on. One thing just led to another, and before the children knew it, the sandbox looked more like a swamp than a sandbox. Wet sand covered their boots and legs, and even their shorts where they had sat in it. Their hands dripped with goop and smudges of dirt crossed their faces. Still they continued on, slopping happily around in the mess, having pushed away all twinges of conscience, until . . .

'Dinner!' Mom's voice called from the back door. Just one word, and suddenly their consciences awoke again. They looked with scared eyes from each others' faces, to their legs, to the sandbox. They had done it again, just like last summer. They should have known better than to even start with a little water, but at the moment it had seemed so harmless . . .

꼶

Jesus also faced many temptations as a child. He would have been tempted by the other village children of his age to join them in their sin. He was tempted to argue with his brothers when they were being unfair, and He was tempted to be disrespectful to his parents when He knew better than them. Just like us, the boy Jesus was tempted to lie when He knew the blame would be cast on Him. He was tempted to be lazy and slow in his work when it was so hot in his father's carpenter shop. And He was tempted to show off when He was better at something than the other children.

Did He give in to these temptations? No, we know that He did not. Not once did Jesus give in to a sinful temptation in his actions, in his words, or even in his thoughts.

Satan was hurling temptations at Jesus, fast and hard, from the moment He was born. Do you know why? Because if Satan could get Jesus to give in to one temptation, Jesus would be a sinner. And you know, don't you, that a sinner could not be the Saviour of a world of sinners?

Now as Jesus grew older, you might think that He was faced with fewer temptations. Satan must have realized by now that Jesus would not commit the smallest sin against God or his neighbour. But this did not happen. Instead, as Jesus grew older, and his time to die on the cross came closer, Satan felt that he was running out of time, and his temptations came even faster and harder than ever before.

See what happened soon after Jesus left his home and family in Nazareth and was baptized by John. He was ready to begin his ministry, to start teaching the people and doing miracles, but first we read that the Spirit took Jesus into the wilderness for a special reason – to be tempted by the devil.

Did God then allow Satan to tempt Jesus? Yes, God did. This is not the first time that this happens in the Bible. God allows his people to be tempted to test them, and to make their faith stronger.

And so after forty days without food in the wilderness, Satan came to Jesus with three clever temptations. First he tempted

Jesus to prove that He was the Son of God: to show off his power by turning stones into bread for himself to eat. Next, Satan used God's own words to tempt Jesus. He wanted Jesus to see if God would really keep Him safe as He had promised. And finally, Satan promised Jesus all the world if He would bow down and worship Satan.

Jesus answered each of Satan's temptations with words from the Bible. The Bible is the only weapon against the Evil One. And the result is? Satan must leave defeated, and 'behold, angels came and ministered unto him' (*Matt.* 4:11).

Through his three years of preaching, Satan continued to tempt the Lord Jesus in many ways. He used the Pharisees to tempt Him, the priests and scribes, ordinary men and women, and even Jesus' own family and disciples.

Shortly before He died, Jesus made his last trip into Jerusalem. The crowds were waiting for Him, but Satan was also there. Look at the people! They are shouting and waving palm branches as Jesus rides in on a young donkey. 'Hosanna!' they cry. 'Become our King and save us from the Romans!'

Jesus had not listened to Satan's other temptation to rule the world, but here Satan came again with the same temptation in a different disguise. Listen to the people calling for the Lord, asking Him to rule them! Will He listen? Will He free them from their enemies? Will the Lord Jesus give in to this temptation? No. For it was not a Saviour from the Romans that the people really needed but a Saviour from their sins. And so He must continue heading to the cross, no matter how hard Satan tried to stop Him.

One of the last temptations that the Lord Jesus faced on earth was when He was hanging crucified on the cross. Then the people mocked Him, 'If thou be the Christ, come down from the cross! He saved others, but himself He cannot save!' Oh, how hard Satan was trying. If Jesus were to come down then, Satan would have won! There would be no Saviour for sinners on earth. 'Come down, Jesus!' he tempts. 'Show the people thy power!'

But no, Jesus ignored all the mocking. He knew they would still not believe in Him, even if He came down from the cross. No, He would finish his work as the suffering Saviour, and rise triumphant from the grave. Satan would not win.

And so you see that being tempted is not a sin, but giving in to temptation is sin. This is what Satan is aiming for. He uses many arguments, coming from others or our own thoughts, to convince us that his temptation is not sin. Think of how Anita was tempted to give in: 'Just a little pond,' came the thought. 'What's so bad about that?' And with that, temptation did turn into sin.

Who then can help us against these powerful temptations of the Evil One? 'God can help us,' I think you will answer, and you are right. God gives his Holy Spirit to those who ask for Him.

The apostle John tells us something about how powerful the Holy Spirit is: 'Greater is he that is in you, than he that is in the world.' The Holy Spirit is greater than Satan who is in the world, and with the Holy Spirit's help, we can stand strong against Satan's temptations. Won't you pray for the Holy Spirit to live in your heart?

17: A BROKEN COFFEE CUP

> *Search me, O God, and know my heart: try me,*
> *and know my thoughts: and see if there be*
> *any wicked way in me.*
> Psalm 139:23, 24

'Well, I'm not inviting her to my birthday party,' Janine informed the other girls.

'Why? What happened?' Kendra asked.

It was recess time, and a group of girls were clustered around the swings.

'You didn't hear about Eileen?' Janine asked in surprise. 'What she did? Well, you know how we're not allowed to touch the things on the teacher's desk? Yesterday, Eileen stayed in for recess. She said she didn't feel well, but I think she just wanted to write on the chalkboard. Well, anyway, she did write on the chalkboards, and then she was playing with the stuff on the teacher's desk, and she broke the teacher's red mug.'

'How did it break?' Kendra asked.

'She bumped it, and it fell on the floor. And then . . .' Janine whispered and looked around to make sure no one else was near, 'she hid it in the bottom of the garbage can!'

'How do you know?' the other girls asked.

'Alex saw her when he was going in to get another soccer ball.'

'Does the teacher know yet?'

'No, but somebody better tell her. Eileen sure won't,' Janine added loudly. 'She doesn't even feel sorry about it!'

'How do you know?' Kendra asked. 'Maybe she talked to the teacher about it after school. She could have told her then that she was sorry.'

'Not!' Janine protested. 'You can tell that she's not sorry at all. Didn't you see her in the hall? I looked at her this morning, and she just gave me a proud smile and walked away.'

'She could have just been trying to be nice,' Kendra tried one more time.

Janine rolled her eyes and said, 'Come on, girls. Let's play army tag.'

❧

Recess was over and the teacher was standing in the doorway to the classroom. In her hand was a different coffee cup from yesterday, a blue one. 'Bring in your Bible Guides,' she reminded the students and walked to her desk, setting down the mug.

'See?!' Janine hissed loudly to Kendra. 'She has a different cup because her other mug is gone! And guess who broke it?' Janine glared over at Eileen's desk where Eileen was already sitting with her books open.

A Broken Coffee Cup

Alex passed the girls in the doorway. 'I told Eileen I saw her put the cup in the garbage, and she said Miss Reinald already knows about it,' he whispered over his shoulder.

Janine smirked at him. 'Guess she'll be in trouble!' she murmured with a smile, but Kendra only frowned.

During the lesson, Miss Reinald needed someone to set up the overhead projector. 'Who is finished questions one to ten?' she asked. Hands flew up quickly as several students were finished and wanted to help. Janine waved her hand wildly in the air. She knew exactly how to set up the projector, but the teacher chose Eileen.

Shyly, Eileen went to get the projector and carefully wheeled it to the front of the classroom. Janine watched with a frown as she plugged it in and pulled down the screen. Why would the teacher choose her? she thought. Especially after she was so bad yesterday. Maybe she hasn't told the teacher about the mug yet.

The students used the diagram on the overhead to take up their map work from yesterday, and then it was time for the Bible lesson.

'Today we have another parable of Jesus,' Miss Reinald began.

'I am sure you have heard this story before, but as we go over it, I want you to think carefully about who each person in the story represents. It is the story of the Prodigal Son. These are the people from the story that I will ask you about.' And she wrote them on the board: the father, the runaway son, the same son when he returns, and the older brother.

Oh, I know this old story, Janine thought to herself. This will be easy. She listened as Miss Reinald explained that Jesus told this story to the Pharisees. They were upset because the Lord Jesus ate at the homes of sinners.

'In the parable, there was a father who had two sons, and the younger son asked for his inheritance. When his father gave it to him, he travelled far away and spent it all. With no money left for food, he got himself a job feeding pigs.

'Finally he realized that even the servants at his father's house had better jobs than he had. So the prodigal son decided to go back home and ask for forgiveness and for a job as a servant. Before he even reached his home, his father came running out to meet him. He was not angry, but very happy to have his son back. He gave him new clothes and shoes and a ring, and he even held a feast for him.

'But when his older brother came in from the field, he was angry. "How come you never have a feast for me?" he asked his father. "Why is my brother being treated so nicely after he was so bad?" And then his father explained that it is right to have a feast and be glad when someone who was lost or bad, is now sorry and has come home again.'

Janine had been listening carefully, and now she looked up at the people listed on the board. Hmmm, this was a little harder than she had thought.

'And so,' Miss Reinald asked the class, 'who does the father represent in this story? Alex?'

'That would be God. God, the Father,' he answered.

'That's right.' Miss Reinald wrote it on the chalkboard. 'And the prodigal son who left with all his money?'

Janine raised her hand, but Miss Reinald called on Kendra.

'I think it might be sinners,' Kendra said, then added, 'Actually, everybody, because everybody sins.'

'That's right,' the teacher nodded. 'Then what about the prodigal son when he returns?'

Janine quickly raised her hand for that one too, but Miss Reinald said, 'Yes, Eileen?'

Janine looked at Eileen to see if she knew the answer. Eileen looked down at her desk and said, 'He would be anyone who is sorry for their sins and asks forgiveness.'

'That's right,' Miss Reinald encouraged, and filled it in on the board. 'Now, the last person we have is the older brother. Who does he represent?'

The class was quiet for a moment, and Janine was thinking hard. She wanted to answer a question. Finally Peter raised his hand. 'Wouldn't he be the Pharisees who came to Jesus? They were angry because Jesus was kind to sinners, just like the older brother was angry because the father was kind to the prodigal son.'

'Good!' Miss Reinald said and wrote 'Pharisees' on the board. 'But I'm still thinking of one more example. Picture the prodigal son returning, his father is running out to meet him, and the older brother is watching angrily. This is the picture of a sinner coming to God, the Lord is welcoming him, and who would be watching angrily?'

Again the class was quiet. Janine was chewing her lip as she thought, and Alex was just raising his hand again, when Janine's hand suddenly shot up.

'Yes, Janine?' Miss Reinald called on her.

'The older brother would be people who, um, don't like to see sinners forgiven,' Janine answered. 'They are people like the Pharisees who think they're so good that only they should go to heaven, and not bad sinners who are sorry for their sins.'

'That is exactly it,' the teacher said and filled in the last blank.

☙

Lunch was over, and Janine was gathering up her books when she overheard the teacher talking to Eileen.

'Thank you for your note this morning, Eileen. I'm glad you told me about the mug right away.' Janine's hands froze at her desk. 'Accidents happen,' Miss Reinald continued, 'and I'm just glad you didn't cut yourself cleaning up the pieces. That was smart to wrap the sharp pieces in paper towel before putting them in the garbage.' And with that, Miss Reinald picked up her coffee cup and walked out of the classroom.

Janine stared down at her binder, and then glanced across the room at Eileen. She remembered all her mean words this morning. She felt just like the older brother in the story of the prodigal son. Eileen had asked forgiveness, but she herself was being like the Pharisees 'who thought they were so good'. Picking up her stack of books, she walked over to Eileen's desk. She knew what she needed to say. ☙

18: TIME'S A-WASTING

> *To every thing there is a season, and a time*
> *to every purpose under the heaven: a time*
> *to be born, and a time to die.*
> Ecclesiastes 3:1, 2

Tick . . . tick . . . tick . . . A little boy sits on the floor looking up at the big old clock hanging on Grandpa's wall. His name is Ben. Hanging down near Ben's feet are two heavy bronze weights. Every day they move down a little lower. That means that soon Grandpa will have to pull the weights up to wind the clock. Ben wishes that he could pull on the chains to bring those weights back up the wall again.

On the face of the clock are two carved hands that point out the time, but the hours are written in Roman numerals. It takes Ben a little while to figure out what the numbers are. Then he remembers. A Roman numeral V means 5, and the small hand is near the V, so it must be almost five o'clock.

Above the sloped roof of the clock is a little bronze man with a hammer. Every hour, the man raises his little hammer and dings out the time. And that is what Ben is waiting for. He wants to see the little man swing his hammer back and

85

strike the metal piece five times. And so he sits and waits and watches. It takes so long for five o'clock to come!

Near the bottom of the clock is a little glass window, and through it, Ben can see another bronze man on a horse swinging back and forth, back and forth. *Tick . . . tick . . . tick . . . tick.* Every second the little rider swings from one side of the window to the other. And every second it gets closer to five o'clock. But, oh, it's so long to wait!

⸙

Have you ever wanted something so badly that you said, 'I can hardly wait!' Maybe you were excited about going on a trip with your family, but you had to wait for two more weeks. Then finally, the day came, and you went on the trip. The trip was fun and you were happy, but soon it was over, and you were back home again.

Then you started looking forward to something else. Three more weeks and it would be your birthday! You could hardly wait. And finally, your birthday came. You were happy, but soon it was over too. And so you became excited about something else: five more weeks and . . . something else would come. Does this happen to you? Do you spend the time God has given you waiting for something fun to come? Do you sit in front of the clock like Ben, wishing that time would hurry up?

Time keeps going at the same pace. When you are young, you think it goes slowly, but when you are old, you will see that your whole life flew by. Do you know when you were born? Do you know what day your birthday is? You do, don't you? Then I have another question for you. Do you know when you are going to die? How long are you going to live?

Until you're ten? Twenty? Fifty? Ninety? You don't know, do you? Only God knows. God chose the day for you to be born on, and He has chosen the day that you will die.

David talks about being born in Psalm 139:14, when he says, 'I am fearfully and wonderfully made.' But David knows that no matter how wonderfully made he was, he will not live forever. Time keeps going by, and soon it will be the day of his death.

And this is what he says about that: 'As for man, his days are as grass: as a flower of the field, so he flourisheth. For the wind passeth over it, and it is gone' (*Psa.* 103:15).

Have you seen the grass grow up fresh and green in the spring? Soon the hot summer sun dries it out, and by the time winter comes, it is brown and dying. That, David says, is what your life is like. It begins like fresh grass, you grow quickly through the summer, and then when the cold winds come, you wither and die.

And so you have a certain amount of time here on earth. The clock keeps ticking, and minutes, hours, days, and years pass by. Every day, you use up more of the time God has given you. And every day, you come closer to the end of your life. Don't wish your time away waiting for something fun to come. Realize instead, that every single day that God gives you is a gift to be used. How are you using this gift?

Tick . . . tick . . . tick . . . There is the sound of gears turning in the clock, and Ben jumps to his feet. The little man swings back his hammer and . . . *ding! . . . ding! . . . ding! . . . ding! . . . ding!* The clock chimes five times, and Ben leaves the room. There is nothing else to see.

87

19: RUNAWAY HORSE: RUNAWAY TONGUE

> *Set a watch, O LORD, before my mouth;*
> *keep the door of my lips.*
> Psalm 141:3

The sun was rising over the treetops of Golden Oaks Ranch, burning off the morning mist and warming the cool barnyard. Twelve-year-old Hannah was standing in the barnyard hopping from foot to foot, partly to get warm and partly from excitement. It was her birthday today, and her parents had promised her weeks ago that she could go horseback riding as a birthday present.

Finally the day had come, and now she stood waiting with her dad. Jill, the owner of the ranch, was saddling up their horses. It seemed to take forever, but at last she came out of the barn leading a small-sized, brown mare. She took her to Hannah, and Hannah was a little disappointed. The horse was not exactly the Black Beauty that she had hoped for. Jill explained, however, that Daisy was a friendly, dependable mare, perfect for beginners.

The horse suddenly seemed big enough to Hannah as she struggled to get her foot into the stirrup and pull herself up. Dad gave her a hand, and there she sat waiting while Jill retrieved two more horses from the barn. Hannah clung to the saddle horn with white knuckles as Daisy shifted her weight from one foot to the other. The ground looked far below from up here, and Hannah felt as though she may lose her balance.

'What if the horse starts going?' she suddenly thought in panic, and looked up for some help. Jill was saddling up her own horse, and Dad had just mounted his own.

'How's it going there?' he called to Hannah.

'Pretty good,' she managed to say.

Just then Jill came over to give her some instructions. 'Here's how you hold the reins. Daisy has a bit in her mouth which is connected to these reins, so when you pull on them, she'll slow down. If you keep reining in, she'll come to a stop. To steer her to the left, you pull gently on the left hand rein, and to turn right, you use the right rein.'

Jill reached down to adjust the stirrups. 'All set? I'll lead the way through the woods and across the road until we get to the meadow path. Then we can let your dad get in a little trotting if he is up to it.'

And so they were off. As they moved down the trail through the fields, Hannah relaxed and enjoyed the feel of jostling along on the mare's wide back. They stopped to look at an old homestead built deep in the woods, and Hannah rubbed Daisy's warm neck as Jill explained some of the history of the spot to Dad. At last they reached the meadow, and after riding for some time there, it was time to turn back.

Hannah was in the rear this time as they came back through the woods. All was going well until they came to a fork in the path. Jill and her dad turned to the left, but Daisy spotted a patch of weedy grass to the right and headed straight for it. Quickly Hannah pulled on the reins to stop Daisy and to turn her back, but the mare was determined to have a little munch on the grass and kept on going.

'Come on! Stop!' Hannah said hesitantly and pulled harder on the reins. Daisy was not convinced that Hannah really meant it, however, and she ambled on over to the weeds. There, she calmly lowered her head and started tearing off weeds with her long lips.

'Dad!' Hannah called out anxiously.

Both Dad and Jill heard her cry and headed back to the fork.

'You're doing great, Hannah,' Jill called out. 'Just pull her head up with the reins; that's it. Now turn her to the left with the reins, and give her a good nudge with your feet.'

Soon Daisy was back on the right trail again, and Hannah could relax a little. On the way home in the truck with Dad, she could even laugh about the stubborn horse.

Back at home, Hannah found her brother Philip in the backyard working on his tree fort. Excitedly she told him about the horseback ride, but when she started telling him how Daisy took the wrong trail in the woods and how she was getting a little scared, Philip interrupted.

'I would've just kept going and cut across through the woods,' he said. 'You're always such a chicken!'

'I am not!' Hannah exclaimed angrily.

'You are too,' Philip laughed.

'Liar! You just come here,' Hannah demanded as he turned to run, and she swung the end of a skipping rope at him.

'Ha! Missed me!' Philip jumped out of the way. Now Hannah was really getting angry, and she quickly grabbed for something else to throw at him.

Philip simply ran away across the yard, but glancing back to see if Hannah was coming, he tripped over a tree root. Losing his balance he fell to the ground.

'Now look what you made me do!' he hollered, and jumping up, he turned and ran after Hannah.

Their chase led them to the garage, where Dad was getting out some tools. Hearing all the commotion he stepped outside to see what was going on.

'Hey! That's enough from you two,' he ordered.

'He called me a chicken!' Hannah quickly panted out.

'Well, she called me a liar and made me fall,' Philip protested.

'Get yourself some rakes and meet me in the back yard,' was Dad's only reply. 'We have some raking and burning to do.'

Soon Hannah was busy raking old leaves out from under the hedge and bushes. She added them to Dad's pile, while Philip dragged over some dead branches that were scattered in the yard by winter storms.

'Isn't this pile a little close to the tree fort?' Philip asked Dad as he got ready to light the pile. 'It's kind of windy and some sparks could blow in the fort.'

Dad glanced up. 'Oh, it's just a little breeze, and what could a few sparks do?' he asked.

'Burn down the tree fort!' Philip answered in surprise. 'Dad!' he exclaimed when it seemed like his dad didn't hear him.

'The sparks could burn down our tree fort! And the tree! And then maybe the shed too!'

Dad looked up at Hannah doubtfully. 'You think so, Hannah? Could a tiny spark start such a big fire?'

Hannah looked from Philip to her dad.

'I think so,' she finally answered. 'If the wind blows on the sparks, they could get a little flame, then start to burn.'

'You're right, Hannah,' Dad said getting up and putting the matches back in his pocket. 'And you too, Philip. A little spark can start a big fire.'

He grabbed a rake and began moving the pile out to the gravel at the end of the driveway. And now the children knew that he had planned all along to burn the pile on the driveway.

'It reminds me of what James said in the Bible,' Dad told them as he again crouched down to light a match. '"Behold, how great a matter a little fire kindleth!", James 3:5.'

'And you know what comes next?' Dad asked Philip. When Philip shrugged, Dad told him, '"And the tongue is a fire, a world of iniquity", James 3:6. Your tongue can start a big fire, just by using little words,' Dad explained.

'Remember what just happened at the house between you and Hannah?' Dad looked at Philip. 'She was trying to tell you about her ride and you interrupted with . . . ?'

'. . . chicken,' Philip admitted. 'I called her a chicken.'

'And I called him a liar,' Hannah admitted in a small voice.

'And what a great fire those small words started!' Dad added. 'You see, James says something else in that same chapter. He says that if we can control our tongues, we can control our whole bodies. Remember what was in the horse's mouth to help you steer, Hannah?'

'A bridle,' she answered quickly.

'Not!' Philip laughed. 'It's a bit, dumb . . .', he stopped suddenly and looked down.

Dad looked at Philip and then continued. 'It is a bit, and if you attach reins to that small bit, you can control the whole horse. In the same way, James says that if you can bridle or control the words that come out of your mouth, you can control your whole body.'

'How about it?' Dad asked the two of them.

'We'll try,' they agreed.

'Good,' Dad answered and poked a few more sticks into the fire. 'But just like a horse will quickly stray from the right path,' he added, 'so will we with our good intentions. We must remember to ask the Lord for help in this every day.' 🐎

20: PULLING WEEDS

> *For God maketh my heart soft, and the*
> *Almighty troubleth me.*
> Job 23:16

It was a warm fall day, and the sun was shining brightly through the coloured leaves. A breeze blew through the yard every once in a while, scattering dry leaves across the driveway. In the corner of the driveway sat a boy. He looked to be about eight or nine years old, and sitting so quietly, you would hardly notice him, except for his feet pushing up gravel into a pile before him.

The smoky smell of leaves being burned could be smelled in the air, and it was the kind of weather that you hope for every Saturday. The kind of weather that makes you want to go for a bike ride, or take a walk down to the creek and dabble in the water, skipping stones and balancing your way across a log.

With the deep blue sky all around and the golden sun beaming down, it was the kind of weather that makes your dog bounce up the moment you open the door, eager for you to take him on a tramp through the woods. At least, this was what Clarence thought. But there he sat in a corner of the driveway, getting dusty from stirring up the gravel.

Why was he sitting there? It was late afternoon, and there was not much time left for all those things he wanted to do. But still he sat, pushing the stones up into a pile and poking the pile with a stick. After a few minutes, he picked up the spade at his side and began hacking at a dandelion weed that had grown in deep below the gravel.

Suddenly he lifted his head as the back door of the house swung open and banged shut. A little boy came flying out with a dog at his heels. 'Hey, Clarence!' he shouted, 'Aren't you gonna come biking with me? Me and Russel are going to the creek and see if we can catch some tadpoles!'

'There aren't any tadpoles in October,' Clarence grumped at his little brother. 'And I ain't coming.'

Russel trotted over to where Clarence was sitting and with eagerly wagging tail, snuffled his nose against Clarence's neck. Clarence pushed the dog away.

'How come?' his little brother Tim asked, wheeling his bike out of the garage.

'I got to pull weeds out of the driveway,' Clarence answered.

'Weren't you supposed to do that yesterday after school?' Tim asked. 'Ma said it'd be real easy 'cause it just rained and the ground was so soft then.'

'Well I wanted to play hockey after school with the other guys, so Ma said I could pull them today if I wanted to. But now they won't come out.' Clarence sighed and got to his feet. 'I only got one corner done, and it's almost supper time. I'm never gonna get done.'

'Well, you'd better hurry up. Dad's gonna be home soon and he said we'd have a game of catch after supper,' Tim advised Clarence. 'You won't be allowed to play if you aren't done. Come on, Russ!' he called to the dog. 'Let's go!'

Clarence watched with envy as Tim went biking down the driveway with Russ bounding along at his side.

'Wish I could go to the creek,' he thought. 'But I've got a million more weeds to pull. I'm never gonna get done. They're so hard to get out! Wish I'd listened to Mom and pulled them out yesterday, after the rain – they came out real easy then. And hockey wasn't much fun anyways.'

With a sigh, Clarence picked up the spade and began digging around another weed.

⁂

You may sometimes hear a Sunday school story or a Bible lesson at school that makes you stop and think. Or you may be listening to the Bible reading at home, and suddenly you realize that you are just like the person in the story. You have done some of the same sins that they have done, you see that you have the same bad heart as they had, and you need the same Saviour that they needed.

This is the Lord's work. He is showing you the sin in your heart. He shows you that you are sometimes unkind, jealous, selfish, unfair, complaining, lazy, proud, careless, or disobedient.

What do you do when you see your sins? Do you confess them and repent of them? Or are you like Clarence and think that another day would be better for pulling weeds? You think,

'Not right now. I just want to finish my book or play a game with everyone else; I don't want to leave and go up to my room by myself. Maybe I'll confess my sins to God tonight when I go to bed, or maybe on Sunday when I have more time. Maybe I'll ask for forgiveness later when I haven't been so bad.' And you quickly forget about these sins that God showed you.

Soon you start thinking, 'I'm not so bad after all! I'm a pretty nice boy or girl, compared to other kids my age. I don't have to confess my sins to God. I'll just thank Him for all the good things He gives me, instead."

But do you know what happens to these sins when you leave them and don't confess them to God? The same thing that happens to the weeds in the driveway. They grow deeper and tougher, and become harder to pull out. It's only after the rain has fallen and softened the earth, that the weeds lose their grip on the ground and are easier to pull out.

And in the same way, when the Lord shows us our sins and makes us sorry for them, that is the best time for us to confess them and repent. That is the time to ask God to stop us from doing them again. If you wait until later, your heart will grow hard again, just like the ground grows hard once the rain stops and the sun comes out.

Pray, then, that the Lord will make your heart soft, that He will show you your sins. Then confess your sins to Him, tell Him about your sorrow over them, and ask Him to help you not to sin. He is ready to hear you. 🦋

21: A TRUE FRIEND

> *Are not five sparrows sold for two farthings,*
> *and not one of them is forgotten before God?*
> Luke 12:6

'Can I skip with you?' Sadie asked a group of girls lining up for a skipping song.

'No, we already have enough people,' one of the girls answered while the others just looked at her silently.

Sadie turned and ran over to Jodie who was just coming out the door with a skipping rope in her hands. 'Jodie! Can I play?' Sadie called.

'Not this recess,' Jodie replied. 'I promised Kayla and the other girls that they could have a turn skipping this recess.' Sadie turned and walked quickly away before Jodie could see the tears welling up in her eyes.

&

Have you ever been left out of a game? Have other kids ever ignored you because they think you're not good enough, fast enough, or smart enough? It hurts when someone leaves you out. You wonder why they won't let you play, and you wonder why they won't be friendly to you.

But still you know that even though some kids might not let you play with them, there are many other people that care about you: your mom and dad, brothers and sisters, aunts and uncles, your cousins, your teachers at school, Sunday school teachers, and even more than all of these, the Lord.

When many people crowded around to hear the Lord Jesus speak, He told them that God cares even for the smallest sparrows. He asked the people, 'Are not five sparrows sold for two farthings, and not one of them is forgotten before God?' (*Luke* 12:6).

In Israel, small birds were sold and bought in the market-place: five birds for just a few cents. These birds were just common, unimportant birds. Sparrows. No one cared about them; no one felt sorry for them. But Jesus tells His listeners that Someone does see those little birds; not one small sparrow is forgotten by Him. And that is His Father in heaven. He cares even for those little birds. What a kind, loving Creator we have! And now, if God cares for such little unimportant birds that do not even have a soul, would He not care for men and women, and boys and girls, much, much more than the birds? Indeed, He does. The Lord Jesus continues and says, 'Fear not therefore: ye are of more value than many sparrows' (*Luke* 12:7).

Do you see how the Lord cares for people? What can you do when you are sad, feeling left out, and hurt by your friends? Can you tell the Lord Jesus about this? If He cares even for the little birds, won't He hear your prayer? Tell Him everything that you need, for your heart, and for your body. Pray to Him every day, and you will find that He is a Friend that will never leave you. He promises this in Hebrews 13:5 where He says: 'I will never leave thee, nor forsake thee.'

♕

School was over for the day, and Sadie was on her way home. The big yellow school bus came to a stop at the end of her driveway. Sadie grabbed her schoolbag and climbed down the steps out of the bus.

'Sadie!' her little sister called from beside the mailbox. 'Sadie! Mom got our bikes out of the shed today, and I'm too big for my tricycle. Let's ask Dad to put your old training wheels on my bike, and then we can bike to the park!'

'Okay!' Sadie called out. A big smile covered her face and she hurried up the driveway with her sister.

That night Sadie climbed into the double bed she shared with her little sister. She wasn't always thankful for her sister, she even called her a pest sometimes, but today Sadie had realized what a good friend her little sister was. The Lord had seen all things that day; He had seen Sadie's tears, and He had provided a friend for her, right here in her family. Before going to sleep, Sadie thanked the Lord for giving her a sister, a friend to love and play with. ♘

# 22: THE KEYSTONE

> *Jesus Christ himself being the*
> *chief cornerstone.*
> Ephesians 2:20b

Click, click, click. The room was quiet except for the sound of Lego pieces snapping together and the occasional, 'Does anyone have a really long piece for me?' or 'Who has a little slanted piece that I can use?'

It was Saturday afternoon, and Mandy and her two brothers, Richard and Bob, were playing Lego in the family room. They were each building a castle in a separate corner of the room. Mandy had all the red Lego blocks, Richard had all the blue, and Bob had all the yellow. The black and white pieces were shared by all of them to make horses and chariots out of.

Mandy's red castle was almost finished. She had spent some extra time making four watch towers and a castle jail, as well as a throne room inside for the king.

Richard had finished his blue castle and was carefully making horses and chariots for his men. He had the only cannon and had set it up on a platform in front of his castle.

Little Bob started his yellow castle, but after finishing only half of the first wall had grown more interested in making horses and chariots. Now his chubby fingers were carefully snapping the little pieces together to make chariots. A long row of colourful and uneven horses already stood in front of his half-built wall.

Soon Mom came in and stood in the doorway to the room. 'Wow!' she exclaimed. 'You have all been very busy! It looks like we've gone back to live a few hundred years ago! Come, get washed up for supper now; you will have to finish another day.'

꙳

The next morning was Sunday, and the family gathered in the family room after church. Mom poured juice for the children, and Dad brought his and Mom's coffee into the family room. Carefully he set the coffee on the table, then headed to the couch, scooping up little Bob and dropping him on his lap.

'So, what was your Sunday school story about today?' Dad asked.

'Jesus,' Bob answered.

'You always say that!' piped up Richard from where he sat with his Lego castle.

'It was about Jesus,' Bob said again nodding his head vigorously.

"That's right," Dad agreed. "Many of the Bible stories are about Jesus.'

'See?' Bob told Richard. 'It was. It was about Jesus and the lepers. He healed them.' Bob climbed down from the couch

The Keystone

to inspect his own half-finished castle. 'We always have stories about Jesus,' he added as he passed Richard. 'Right, Dad?'

'That's right, Bob,' Dad agreed. 'In the first Sunday school class you study about the life of Jesus, so that's why all the stories are about Jesus.

'Actually, Richard,' Dad went on, picking up his coffee. 'All of your Sunday school stories are about Jesus too.'

Richard looked up, surprised, and put down the chariot he was holding. 'What do you mean?' he asked Dad. 'We're studying about King David right now, not about Jesus.'

'Well,' Dad answered, 'in a way, the whole Bible is about Jesus – not just the New Testament stories about Jesus' life, but even all the Old Testament stories. Even though those stories about Noah and Abraham, Ruth, and David don't say the name of Jesus in them, they are still about Him.'

Seeing Richard's puzzled frown Dad continued.

'Why do you think those stories are in the Bible?' he asked Richard.

'I don't know . . .' Richard began, then thought for a moment. 'They're telling about the start of the world and the flood and stuff, and about the Israelites.'

'That's right,' Dad said.

'And I know why else they're in the Bible!' Mandy piped up from the other end of the couch where she was sitting with a book. 'Those stories tell why Jesus had to come.'

'What do you mean?' Richard asked Mandy.

'Well,' she answered, 'the first story is how the world started and Adam and Eve sinned and everyone was bad so a flood had to come. Then the people were bad again after the flood and got all different languages, then God chose Abraham to serve Him, and after him came Isaac, and Jacob, and then the Israelites. Then there's stories about David to show that Jesus would come from his family. So the stories go all through the Israelite kings till Jesus is born!'

'That's right,' Dad agreed. 'So all the stories in the Old Testament are there to tell about the promise of Jesus coming and the way that He would come. And all the stories in the New Testament are there to tell about Jesus' life and how the church should live after He ascended to heaven. The church should now be waiting for Jesus to come again for the second time. You see? Jesus is the centre of the Bible. Does that make sense, Richard?'

Richard looked up from the castle he was playing with. 'Yeah, I get it,' he answered. 'All the first stories are telling about Jesus coming to be the Saviour, and the rest are about after He comes.'

'That's right,' Dad said and bent over to look at Richard's castle. 'That's a pretty neat castle you've built there,' he commented. 'You've even got an arched gateway leading inside.'

'Yeah,' Richard answered without looking up. 'A gateway with an arched top is stronger than a straight gateway. We learned that in science. And my castle's got to be strong to defend itself against the enemies.'

'Why is an arch stronger?' Bob asked crouching down to peer at Richard's gateway. 'Help me build one too!'

'Well, this isn't a true arch,' Richard answered, 'but it's still pretty strong. Here, I'll show you why an arch doorway is stronger than a straight doorway."

Richard got up from the floor and looked through the desk drawer to find a pencil and a scrap of paper. Dad and Bob gathered around the table to watch him draw. Even Mandy put down her book to come see. Mom, just coming into the room, also came over to the table.

Quickly, Richard drew a castle wall with a straight-topped doorway opening into it. 'See this doorway?' he asked. 'If you put lots of pressure right above the door, all the weight will push on the straight beam that's across the top of the doorway, and it will crack.'

Now Richard drew another doorway next to it, this time in an arched shape. 'A true arch,' he explained, 'has stones that start from the ground on each side of the door and are built up. Then when the builder gets near the top, he cuts the stones on an angle so that the top of the door curves into an arch.' Carefully Richard drew the stones leading up on each side of the doorway and curving over the top.

'Then,' Richard continued, 'the builder puts in the last stone which goes right in the middle of the top of the doorway, and that stone holds all the other ones up. That stone is called the *keystone*. If you didn't have that stone in the centre, the two sides of the doorway would fall in.'

'Okay,' Mandy said, 'that doorway is built differently, but why is it stronger than a normal doorway?'

''Cause look,' Richard showed her. 'See? If you put lots of weight here on the rounded top of the doorway, the arch won't crack like the other doorway. The slanted sides of the keystone press the weight into the next stones, which push into the next stones, all the way down into the ground. And the ground isn't going to crack,' Richard finished.

Bob laughed. 'Of course not!' he said. 'Unless there's an earthquake!'

'So, we've all learned something!' Mom said looking over Richard's shoulder at his drawing.

'You know something,' Dad said to Richard. 'You said that without that keystone in the centre, the sides of the doorway would fall in. I was just thinking that that is exactly what the Lord Jesus is in the Bible. He is the keystone. If He was not in the Bible, all those other stories would mean nothing. But with Jesus as the keystone, as the centre of the Bible, all the Bible stories build together to make a strong, sure doorway: the doorway of salvation.' ❧

23: THE CHARACTER OF A KING

For thou art not a God that hath pleasure in wickedness . . . for thou, LORD, wilt bless the righteous.
Psalm 5:4, 12

It was a dreary day in February; the sun refused to shine and grey clouds had settled over the sky as if to stay. Mandy, Richard, and Bob were playing with their Lego set-ups in the family room. They had each built a castle last week: Mandy with the red blocks, Richard with the blue, and little Bob, well, he had started building with the yellow, but he had soon given up.

Now he was lying next to Mandy's castle on the floor and asking her to explain all the parts. And so Mandy tells him what each room is and how it is used. Most of the rooms are small and empty, but the throne room is big and has some people in it. Bob wants to know the name of each of the Lego people and what they are doing. And so Mandy names her people, and as she tells the story of her castle, Bob can almost see it happening right before his eyes.

Why don't you lie down next to him there on the family-room floor? Then you can see in the castle doorway too and hear about what is happening inside.

'What's that square thingy on the wall right inside the door?' Bob asks Mandy and points it out with his chubby finger.

'Oh, that's all the king's laws,' Mandy tells him. 'They tell the bad things that you must not do in the king's country, and they tell what will happen to you if you are bad.'

'Why? Why will something happen to you if you're bad?' Bob wants to know. 'Is the king mean?'

'No,' Mandy says. 'He's not being mean, he's just being fair.'

'Who is this lady who just came in the door?' Bob asks pointing to an old woman who is just inside the castle door. 'Is she reading the laws on the wall?'

'No,' Mandy answers. 'That's Matilda. She's an old woman that is coming to the king for help. Her house burned down in a fire, and all her money and stuff burned too, and she has no one to help her. The king is very kind, and he will go him-self to look at Matilda's house and give orders to have a new one built. In the meantime, he will give her a room to sleep in in his castle. But she doesn't know that yet, and so she is waiting for her turn to see the king.'

'Then he really is a nice king,' Bob says and nods seriously. 'She doesn't need to be scared to ask for help. You made your castle pretty fancy, Mandy,' he continues. 'It's all yellow gold inside with neat designs. Are those supposed to be jewels carved in the throne?'

'Yeah,' Mandy says. 'And see the tiles on the floor? They're all made out of marble. And see the king on the throne? He has the nicest, richest clothes and his whole throne is made out of gold.'

'He must be a pretty rich king,' Bob comments.

'Yup,' Mandy agrees. 'He owns everything in his kingdom, but lets his people use what they need to live. He is very powerful. See that man lying on the floor in front of the throne?' she asks.

'Yeah,' Bob looks with big eyes. 'Who is that man who is holding his chain? Is he mean?'

'No,' Mandy tells him. 'That man is Ramin. He is one of the king's soldiers. The man lying on the floor was a really bad man who broke the king's law about stealing. He begged the king for another chance to be good, and the king let him go free after doing some work for him. But guess what? He wasn't good; he went right back out and started stealing again. So now he is in big trouble. He won't escape his punishment this time!'

'Look over here.' Mandy points to the arm of the throne. 'This is the king's sceptre.' Picking up a golden rod from the throne, she shows it to Bob. 'No one may use this sceptre except the king. And this is his golden goblet and plate. They are also only allowed to be used by the king.'

'They're special things,' Bob agrees, 'not for normal people.' He rolls over on to his side and is about to get up when he spots one more Lego person just outside the castle.

'Who is that boy over there with the horse?' he asks Mandy, and points to a Lego person that is leading a horse towards the king's stable.

'This boy?' Mandy asks. 'This is Jonquel. He is really happy right now because the king has forgiven him. You see, the king found out that someone in his castle was taking his food supplies and selling them at the market. The king ordered that this person should be caught and punished.

'This boy Jonquel was the one doing it. He worked in the king's kitchen, but wanted money to buy a horse of his own. But when he knew he might get caught, Jonquel came before the king and admitted what he had done. The king looked so stern, and he was so scared. But since he had come and confessed what he had done, the king forgave him and didn't punish him. Jonquel was so happy and thanked the king, and then the king even made him a stable boy! Now he helps take care of the king's horses,' Mandy ends her explanation.

'Man,' little Bob sighs in wonder. 'I wish I could really visit your king in his castle. I'd have to be on my best behaviour, though, like Mom always says. Just like in church, you know? No whisperin' and pay attention, because it's God's house.'

Mandy stretches and gets up from her knees. 'That's right,' she agrees. 'The Lord is a powerful and fair and kind King too. That's why we always have to be respectful in His house.'

'Reverent,' Bob adds. 'That's what my Sunday school teacher says. We have to be reverent.'

The Lord is a far more powerful, fair and kind king than any king that ever lived on earth. You would show great respect if you visited a real king's palace. How do you go into the Lord's house each Sunday? 🐛

24: THE GOOD SHEPHERD

> *He shall feed his flock like a shepherd: he shall*
> *gather the lambs with his arm, and carry them in his*
> *bosom, and shall gently lead those that are with young.*
> Isaiah 40:11

It is early morning in Israel. The sun is just rising over the green pastures, and in the distance a boy can be seen making his way over the hills. In his hand is a long staff with a crook in the end. He is using it as a walking stick to help him up the steep places. This boy is a shepherd. Every morning as the sun rises, he also rises to take the family's flock out to pasture. His older brothers help his father with sowing, plowing, and harvesting crops in the fields. But being the youngest, he has the job of caring for the sheep.

See the shepherd boy coming over the hill. He is leading the sheep to water. Running through the valley is a stream, but the sheep will not drink from running water. That is why he is taking them down to where the stream settles into a still pool of water. There the sheep can drink as much as they need.

The sheep can see the water now, but before they can reach the pool, they have to pass down a steep rocky place in the hill. One by one and two by two they bound down over the rough place as the shepherd boy coaxes them on. At last they are all down, all except one.

A young sheep stands at the top of the hill and raises its head to bleat out a cry of fear. It is afraid to come down the steep place. The boy calls the sheep by name, but still it hesitates. At last the boy reaches for his leather sling, chooses a smooth stone, and swinging the sling above his head by its two strings, suddenly lets one string loose. The stone flies high up the hill and lands with a clatter right behind the sheep. Startled, the sheep bounds forward and clambers awkwardly down the rocky hill.

The shepherd boy settles down on a rock to wait while the sheep are drinking their fill. Once they have enough, they move away to feed on the thick green grass that grows in this area. And the boy also is hungry. He lays his staff alongside the rock and leans his rod against his knees. Reaching into his scrip, a bag made of dried skin, he pulls out some olives and dried fruit. He will keep the bread and cheese for later in the day.

Time passes, and soon a neighbouring flock can be seen coming over the hills. This pool of water is shared by several Israelite farmers, and soon the area is filled with a mixture of sheep: the shepherd boy's herd, and the neighbour's herd. The sheep mill about, eating the rich grass, and some begin to wander farther and farther along the stream.

At last the boy rises to go. He gathers up his staff and rod and calls for his sheep to follow. The sheep lift their heads, and hearing their master's voice, come to him. He counts them as they come. Two are missing. They have followed the stream deeper into the valley and cannot hear his voice.

Quickly, the boy leaves his flock by the pool and runs along the stream looking for the sheep. Rounding a group of rocks, he sees them, feeding in some long grass. He calls urgently to the foolish sheep, so foolish to have left the safety of the flock and the protection of the shepherd. Here they were wandering in the open, exposed to wild animals.

The two sheep hear his voice, and come to him, willing to follow him back to the flock. And so, with every sheep accounted for, they leave the green grass of this area to find other pastures.

Their way now leads over sandier ground, and bushes dot the land. There is some underbrush and trees along the way, and the shepherd boy becomes very watchful now. He pauses suddenly, as he hears a rustle in the bushes. His hand grips his rod tightly, a short thick club with spikes driven in one end. There could be a wild animal prowling nearby, looking for a stray sheep.

Waiting silently, his eyes move back and forth scanning the long grass and bushes. His other hand moves to his sling and fits a stone into its leather pouch. The danger passes however, as no animal appears to challenge the shepherd or sheep. Once more the boy leads his flock on.

At noon the shepherd rests in the shade from the midday sun, and when the afternoon shadows grow long, he leads his flock back to the watering place. There they are refreshed, and as they make their way back to the sheepfold, he calls to them. He encourages the slow and tired ones, and gathers the smallest lamb up into his arms to carry it home.

At last, safely back at the sheepfold, he counts his sheep as they pass one by one into the narrow doorway. And there, huddled together within its stone walls, the sheep can sleep safely through the night. The shepherd will lie down in the open doorway. He will keep the sheep safe. For no thieves or animals will get past him.

૪

What an important job a shepherd has! How much work it takes to feed and protect a flock of sheep. Jesus tells us that He is the Good Shepherd. Just as a shepherd in Israel looks after his sheep, so Jesus will take good care of His people. He will give them joy and peace in their hearts, He will feed their souls with words from the Bible, He will comfort them when they are sad, give them strength when they are weak, and He is preparing a place for them in His heavenly sheepfold where they will be safe for ever.

This Good Shepherd is calling you by name. Are you one of His flock? Or are you still wandering away from Him? Won't you give up your own ways and follow Him?

25: NO ROOM

'Go ahead, kids,' Mom called as she held open the door to the nursing home. 'Grandma will be waiting for you. I should be back in an hour,' she added as Daniel, Ariel, Ellen and Joel filed in the door past her.

'Where are you going?' Ellen asked as Mom stepped back out into the cold.

'I just have to pick up some food for Christmas dinner, drop off Dad's suit at the drycleaner's, and get a gift for Aunt May. Be good,' Mom added bending to kiss Ellen.

'Come!' little Joel commanded tugging on Ariel's hand. 'Let's see G'andma.' The four of them trooped down the hall, smiled at the lady behind the desk, then climbed the stairs to the second floor. There they headed straight to Room 38 and knocked on the door.

'Oh! Come in! Come in!' Grandma said warmly, opening the door. 'I was waiting for you. Look at your rosy cheeks!' she said bending to kiss Joel. 'It must be cold out there! Here, you can leave your coats on this chair.' Soon the children were all settled around the table with chocolate milk and chewy chocolate-chip cookies.

Daniel and Ariel told Grandma about the projects they were working on at school. Ellen told about the funny dream she had had last night. And Joel pulled up his pant leg to show Grandma the big bruise he got from falling down the stairs. Then Grandma showed the children some new pictures from the Thanksgiving dinner they had had together.

'So, what special day is coming up?" Grandma asked Joel. He thought for a moment.

'Wednesday!' he said at last. The other children laughed.

'Christmas!' Ellen told him. 'A few more days and it will be Christmas.'

'That's right,' Grandma agreed, 'so why don't we come sit by the rocker and I'll read you the Christmas story. You can never hear it enough. Daniel, will you get the Bible from that shelf? Thank you.'

And Grandma settled herself into the rocker with the children gathered around her. 'Here we are,' she said, flipping the pages, 'Luke 2. "And it came to pass in those days, that there went out a decree from Caesar Augustus, that all the world should be taxed."'

Grandma stopped to explain what she had read, and then continued on with Mary and Joseph arriving in Bethlehem. 'And so it was, that, while they were there, the days were accomplished that she should be delivered. And she brought forth her firstborn son, and wrapped him in swaddling clothes, and laid him in a manger; because there was no room for them in the inn.'

'Why was there no room for them in the inn?' Ellen interrupted Grandma's reading.

'Well,' Grandma replied, 'all the beds were full already, and no one would give their bed to Mary and Joseph and baby Jesus. They wouldn't find some room for them anywhere in the inn, so they had to go out to the stable with the animals.'

'That's mean,' little Joel piped up.

'I would have given my bed,' Ellen added.

'You would have?' Grandma asked smiling. 'You would have made room for the Lord Jesus?' At Ellen and Joel's nods, Grandma continued the reading with the story of the shepherds. She then closed the Bible and asked them a question.

'We can't give the baby Lord Jesus our bed, because He was born a long time ago. But do you think we can still make room for the Lord Jesus?'

The children all looked at her, thinking. Then Daniel and Ariel slowly nodded. 'I think we can have things about Jesus in our house,' Ariel said, 'like a Bible.'

'Yeah, and read it too,' Daniel agreed. 'Like, we can't let Jesus really into our house through the door, but we can think about Him and talk to Him.'

'That's right,' Grandma agreed. 'We don't have to make a real room or bed for the Lord Jesus in our house, but we have to make room for Him in our lives.'

'How do you make room in your life?' Ellen asked.

'Well, you need to make time for Him,' Grandma answered. 'Your life will be full of things to do, but you need to make space, time, for the Lord Jesus. You need time to think about Him, read about Him, pray to Him — '

'And sing about Him!' Ariel added. 'We always sing from the Psalter right after supper.'

'And before bed we sing our song for Sunday school,' Ellen added.

Grandma nodded, smiling.

'Me too! I sing too!' Joel added.

'That's good,' said Grandma, rubbing his head. 'So now do you see how we have to make room for the Lord Jesus too?'

Daniel listened thoughtfully as Grandma went on. 'If your life was the inn that Mary and Joseph went to, would there be a sign on the door of your life that said, "No room!"? Or is there room in your life for the Lord Jesus?'

The children thought about this, and watched as Grandma carefully put the Bible away. They had a few more minutes before Mom would be back, so they started a game of Chinese Checkers.

Soon Mom's head poked in the door. 'Hi Mom!' she called out to Grandma. 'Come along; get your coats on,' she said to the kids. 'Did you have a nice visit? It took longer than I thought, and we'd better hurry, 'cause I've got to get supper on, then you kids have to get washed up before your cousins come over.'

The next few days were busy ones, wrapping gifts for the family get-together next week, cleaning the house for all the visiting that would be done between Christmas and New Year, and baking all sorts of cookies, squares, and loaves for the family and visitors. Mom seemed to be in five places at once, and the children scurried around helping her. There would be time to sit down when it was all over, Mom told them, 'So practise your songs for Sunday school, help me change the sheets on the bed, clean out the toy cupboard for your cousins that are coming over . . .'; it seemed the list went on and on.

At last it was the day before Christmas. Mom was in the kitchen making up trays of baked goods. The crockpot was bubbling on the counter, and little Joel was amusing himself by smearing some spilt gravy over the counter with a spoon. Ariel came into the kitchen to ask Mom where she wanted the clean laundry. 'What are we all doing tomorrow?' she asked Mom.

'Yeah,' echoed Ellen right behind her. 'What are we doing after the Sunday school program?'

'Well, we'll have to get up in time to be ready for church,' Mom answered. 'Then we'll have Uncle Rob and Aunt Sue over for dinner. They'll come with us to the Sunday school program. We'll have to bring clothes with us to change into, so we can head straight from the program to Uncle Paul and Aunt Trina's farm.'

'See G'andma?' little Joel stopped smearing the gravy to ask.

'No, honey, not tomorrow,' Mom answered.

'But when will Daddy be reading the Christmas story and telling about Jesus being born?' Ariel asked.

'Oh, you'll hear a story at the Sunday school program,' Mom told her.

'But what about Joel? He doesn't get it; someone has to explain it to him,' Ariel continued.

'Yeah, and when are we gonna sing Christmas songs and do more stuff about Jesus?' Ellen asked. 'We hafta have room for Him, Grandma said.'

'Well, maybe we can all sing at Uncle Paul and Aunt Trina's,' Mom suggested.

'We probably won't,' Daniel said, coming in the door, 'We never do. The kids always want to just have snowball fights, then play in the haymow.' Daniel dropped down into one of the kitchen chairs.

'It seems like we're too busy to even have Christmas, Mom,' Daniel continued. 'You used to read us stories and sing by the organ, but now everything is so busy. Even Dad's always busy.'

'Yeah, maybe we have a sign on our door that says "No Room",' Ellen suggested. 'No room for Jesus 'cause we're too busy.'

Mom stopped and put down the tray she was wrapping. She looked at the children for a moment silently. She had been too busy. She wasn't making time and room for the Lord Jesus in Christmas. And her children saw that.

'Maybe you're right,' she told them. 'We are too busy. Mom has been too busy. Rushing around, and for what? We do need to make room for Jesus.'

'Daniel,' Mom went on, 'Why don't you run and ask Dad if he can stay home tonight and meet with Mr Rawlins next week? We'll still go to Uncle Paul and Aunt Trina's tomorrow, but we can stop by and pick up Grandma to come over for lunch and the Sunday school program first. She's going to Aunt Rachel's later in the day, but I know she'd love to have lunch here and see your program. Let's finish these trays, then no more work today. The rest can wait.'

A smile lit the children's faces as Daniel ran off to ask Dad, and Ariel and Ellen went to find the Children's Story Bible to read from this afternoon. Joel stood on the chair and waved his dripping spoon in the air. 'G'andma's coming!' he announced happily.

Now what about you? Grandma asked the children a question that you can also answer for yourself. 'If your life was the inn that Mary and Joseph went to, would there be a sign on the door of your life that said, "No room!"? Or is there room in your life for the Lord Jesus?'

26: THE LAST MARRIAGE

All things are ready;
come unto the marriage.
Matthew 22:4

There they stood at the front of the church, three bridesmaids, their dresses bright, next to the three ushers and groom. The little flower girl stood there too, nervously clutching her basket of flowers. Then the music swelled, and all eyes turned to the back of the church. The groom stood still, his eyes fixed on the doorway at the end of the aisle. Anticipation was written on every face.

At last the bride appeared, dressed in white, holding her father's arm. The audience stood as the processional began. Smiles lit every face, and cameras flashed as the bride slowly made her way to the front of the church. A smile lit her face too, but her eyes were on the groom, the young man waiting for her at the end of the aisle. This was the day she had long been planning for. This was the hour she had long been waiting for. This was the moment she had long been dreaming of.

At last she reached the end of the aisle and the minister turned to her father, 'Who gives this woman to this man?' he asked.

'By the grace of God, her mother and I do,' her father replied, and the groom stepped forward to take her arm.

❦

Sarah was sitting quietly in the audience, watching everything that happened. Two months earlier they had received a large white envelope in the mail. Opening it, Mom had pulled out a beautiful card with words written in silver ink.

'What is it? What is it?' she had asked tugging on Mom's sleeve.

'It's an invitation to your cousin Lisa's wedding,' Mom had told her. 'She's getting married on August 7, and we're all invited!'

Sarah's face lit up with a big smile. 'So I get to go too?' she asked with surprise.

'Yes,' Mom told her.

'Oh boy! I can hardly wait!' Sarah exclaimed. 'How many more days will it be? Will Lisa be wearing a wedding dress like we saw on Rachel's pictures? Does Lisa know we're going to come to the wedding?'

'Let's see,' Mom thought a moment. 'The wedding is in about sixty days. Do you think you can wait that long? And I don't think Lisa's dress will look just like Rachel's, but it probably will be white! And see this little card and envelope with the invitation? That's where we write our answer on, to tell Lisa that we're coming.'

'Now, I know you have a hundred more questions, but I need to get supper into the oven, so why don't you run and tell your sister about the wedding invitation?' suggested Mom.

'Okay!' Sarah agreed running from the kitchen. 'Elise! Elise! Guess what? We're going to a wedding!'

That night after supper, Sarah watched Mom fill out the reply card that told Lisa that they were coming. Sarah helped lick the envelope shut. 'Are you sure you want to go?' Mom teased her, 'because you can't change your mind once I've mailed it!'

'M-o-m!' Sarah said. 'Of course I want to go!'

Now, two months later, the wedding day had come at last. And here was Sarah, sitting in church, watching it all. The wedding was far more beautiful than she had imagined. The music and all the flowers. And the bridesmaids! She hadn't expected them to be in the wedding. And the little flower girl – she looked so cute.

But Lisa looked the most beautiful of all, Sarah thought. When she was older, she would get married and have a wedding dress just like Lisa's, she decided.

❦

Have you ever been to a wedding? Has your family ever received a wedding invitation in the mail? How exciting that must have been! Dad and Mom had to check the calendar to make sure you could all go, and then the reply card had to be sent back to the bride. 'Yes!' it said, 'we all can come to the wedding!' Two more months. It must have seemed a long time to wait.

But maybe you haven't ever received a wedding invitation in the mail, or you have never gone to a wedding before. Well, I would like to tell you about a wedding that is coming up, and that you have been invited to. The Lord tells us about this wedding in the Bible.

It is the wedding between the Lord Jesus and His people. You have heard about the Last Day when the Lord Jesus will come to judge all people. And you know how those who do not love the Lord will be punished forever, and those who do love and serve the Lord will go to be with Him in heaven. Well, God calls these people that love the Lord Jesus, His Bride.

The Lord Jesus is the Bridegroom, and His people will be married to Him on the Last Day when they join Him in heaven. Read what the Lord says in Revelation 19:7,9 (the Lamb that is mentioned in these verses is the Lord Jesus): 'Let us be glad and rejoice, and give honour to him: for the marriage of the Lamb is come, and his wife hath made herself ready . . . Blessed are they which are called unto the marriage supper of the Lamb.'

'But I never got an invitation to this wedding of the Lord Jesus', you may think. 'I was not invited to be a part of the bride of the Lord Jesus.' Actually, you have been! Has your dad or mom, your Sunday school teacher, or your minister ever told you about the Lord Jesus? Has anyone ever told you that you have a sinful heart and that the Lord Jesus invites sinners to come to Him for a new heart? If you have heard this many times, then you have also been invited many times to become a part of the Lord Jesus' bride.

Listen to what the Lord Jesus says in Matthew 22:4: 'All things are ready; come unto the marriage.' And again, in

John 6:37: 'Him that cometh to me I will in no wise cast out.' You are invited to come to Him, and those who do, will one day be joined with Him forever at His marriage feast in heaven.

What have you done with your invitation? 🐛

27: OF DOGS AND NEWSPAPERS

'It's all right; he doesn't bite,' the man called from the front door and spoke to the dog. At his command, the big black dog halted in the middle of the lawn.

Timidly Reuben headed up the walk, newspaper in hand. Keeping his eye on the dog, he handed the newspaper to the man and hurried back down the steps to his bike. Hitching his newspaper bag up on his shoulder, he pedalled off. Casting a glance over his shoulder, he saw the dog still standing there, staring after him.

It was a few minutes before his heart slowed down and his body relaxed. By then he had delivered five more newspapers and was working his way back down the other side of the street.

'Why did those people sign up for the newspaper anyway?' Reuben muttered to himself. 'It was bad enough just passing their house, but now I've got to deliver there every day!' He had often seen the dog dozing on the driveway, but had been careful not to look too closely or attract its attention as he biked by. But now? Now he had to walk right up to that front door. Reuben shuddered and hurried to finish his route.

'All done?' Mom called from the kitchen as Reuben let the back door slam shut. 'That was quick. You can get started on your homework because supper will be a few minutes yet.'

The tricky business of dividing improper fractions soon put all thoughts of the dog out of his head. In fact, Reuben didn't even think of the dog again until the next day when he was riding the bus home from school. A feeling of dread crept into his heart as the bus pulled up to his bus stop. 'I hope that dog is locked in the house,' he muttered fiercely to himself.

And his hope seemed to come true. Cautiously he approached the house, newspaper in hand. Silently, without the slightest rattle or clang, he lowered his bike to the ground. Almost on tiptoe, he crept up the walk and slipped the newspaper into the mailbox. A soft thud sounded from the closing lid and *Woo-woo-woo-woof!* A tremendous bark came echoing down the front hall.

With a jerk, Reuben whirled around and raced down to his bike, his heart pounding wildly.

The next two days were the same. By the fourth day, Reuben was determined not to let the dog hear him. Instead of starting at the beginning of his newspaper route, he started at the dog's. This way he would be a little earlier and the dog wouldn't expect him yet.

With his body a tense coil of nerves, Reuben eased himself up the front porch steps and slowly, so painfully slowly, slipped the newspaper into the mailbox. Holding his breath, he lowered the lid and crept back down the steps.

No barking.

'I did it!' Reuben grinned to himself as he pedalled away. 'Ha! That solves that problem.'

And it did solve the problem, until one day Reuben got the fright of his life. Quietly he climbed the porch steps, and silently he slipped the newspaper in the box. But just as he was heading down the driveway to his bike, a tremendous barking came from a black form hurtling around the side of the house.

The sound seemed to jolt Reuben off his feet. In one mad leap he sprang on to his bike and pushed off. Pedals flailed and gravel flew as he spun on to the road. His only thought was of escaping the gaping pink mouth and flashing white teeth coming after him.

And escape he did, for reaching the end of the driveway, the dog screeched to a halt, to continue his barking from there. It was a long minute before his long legs turned and carried him back up the driveway to where he flopped lazily in the sun.

As for Reuben, five houses later he was still shaking and could still hear the echo of that bark rattling through his head.

Reuben had not yet told anyone about the new house on his paper route. After all, he was twelve years old and shouldn't be afraid of a dog. At least, that's what he told himself the whole way home from school the next day.

I just can't deliver that newspaper today, he told himself as he was setting out with his bike. That dog is going to take my arm off one of these days! People shouldn't be allowed to keep such a vicious dog. Angry and worried, Reuben stopped at the newspaper drop-off point and loaded the papers into his bag.

But he's not vicious, Reuben reminded himself, the man said so. He's just doing his job: barking at strangers. And besides, added his conscience, they paid for their newspaper, and it's your job to deliver it. The dog will probably be inside, so just ring the doorbell, and tell them what happened yesterday. Ask them to keep their dog inside until you've delivered their paper.

With these thoughts swirling in his head, Reuben swung the heavy bag over his shoulder with a grunt. He glanced up at the grey sky. It matched his grey mood. Nervous, but determined, he headed straight towards the dreaded house. There's no way I'm ringing their doorbell, he decided. I'll get past that dog somehow.

He saw the dog at the same moment that it saw him. For a second they stared at each other. Then in one leap the dog was off the porch and barrelling across the lawn. Reuben didn't stop to think. He didn't even stop his bike. Yanking a newspaper out of his bag, he rolled it up in one hand and threw it down the driveway. Before the dog could reach him, he was gone, pedalling off to the next house with his heart in his throat.

It was not until a few houses down that Reuben started thinking of the newspaper instead of the dog. It was most likely spilled open somewhere on the driveway . . . unless the dog had chewed it up. That is not the way you are paid to deliver newspapers, his conscience told him.

Yeah, but it's their own fault for letting that dog outside, he argued. And angrily, he pushed the incident out of his mind.

Of Dogs and Newspapers

Splat! Split! Splat! Big drops of rain darkened the pavement beneath his tires. Reuben yanked up his hood with one hand and pedalled faster towards home. He was just coming into the driveway when the clouds poured out a great gush of rain. Throwing up the garage door, he shoved his bike inside and dashed into the house.

'Wow! It's really coming down,' Dad said as Reuben pulled off his dripping coat. It was just an innocent remark, but Reuben froze. The newspaper. Lying on the driveway. In the rain. Slowly Reuben pulled off his shoes and headed to the kitchen for supper.

All that evening, his conscience accused him. Look what you've done! They're not going to be happy with a dripping newspaper on their driveway. They're going to call the newspaper office, and you'll lose your job. You should have rung the doorbell long ago and asked them to keep their dog inside when you delivered. You took a shortcut today, and now you'll pay for your mistake.

Reuben went to bed early that night with a head-ache. Over breakfast and during recess, he worried about what to do. After school he still hadn't come to a decision as he biked up to the dog's house. Pausing, he balanced on his bike at the end of the driveway. No dog. Slowly Reuben walked up to the porch. Still no dog. 'Ring the doorbell!' his conscience told him as he slipped the newspaper into the box. 'Tell them you're sorry about yesterday, and ask them to keep the dog inside.' But no, silently he slipped back down the sidewalk to his bike. With heavy feet and a heavy heart he finished up his paper route.

Supper was over and Reuben was working on his homework.

'Do you know your memory verse for tomorrow?' Mom asked as she walked by.

'Yeah,' Reuben said. 'We have two this week. They are both about loving God. John 14:15: If ye love me, keep my commandments, and 1 John 4:18: There is no fear in love; but perfect love casteth out fear.'

'Good,' said Mom. 'Those are words to keep in your heart. It's very easy to say we love the Lord, but then we have to look at our actions. Do we keep His commandments? Do we even want to keep His commandments? That is the test that shows if we love Him. And if we do love Him, we will not be afraid of what others think. We will try to always keep His commandments.'

Mom's words sank deep into Reuben's heart. 'If ye love Me, keep my commandments,' pressed into his mind. He had been too afraid to face his fear and too embarrassed to admit his fear. He had deliberately done wrong, and there was only one way to make it right.

Slowly, dragging his feet, Reuben headed downstairs to the family room. This felt like the hardest thing he had done in his life.

'Dad?' he said. 'I've got to go talk to someone on my paper route, but it's getting dark outside. Can you come with me?'

In a few minutes, the two of them were biking down the street. Already the weight seemed to be lifting from Reuben's heart. Just telling Dad about the dog and the wet newspaper had been a relief.

Reuben led the way to the house, and Dad waited on the driveway with his bike. Somehow the thought of the dog was not as scary with Dad waiting in the shadows behind him.

Still, it was a nervous finger that pressed the doorbell. *Woo-woo-woo-woof!* A tremendous bark came echoing down the hall. In a moment the door opened, and the dog's owner stood before him.

Hesitantly Reuben told the man about the wet newspaper and how it came to be lying on the driveway. As he spoke, his eyes kept drifting down to the dog who snuffled at him from behind his master's legs.

A smile crossed the man's face as Reuben finished. 'I was once afraid of dogs too,' he admitted. 'But see this big guy? He's a people lover. He greets everyone on the driveway and would welcome anyone into our house. Good thing robbers don't know that. He sounds fierce enough to eat someone whole . . . until you look at his tail. See?'

The dog seemed to know they were talking about him, for just as Reuben leaned to the side to get a look, he gave a deep bark. Reuben jumped, then laughed nervously. At last he leaned again to get a look at his tail. Sure enough, it was wagging happily.

'He's just saying hello and welcome,' the man smiled. 'And don't worry about the paper. These things happen. We appreciate you coming by though. Have a good night.'

And with that the door closed.

What a sigh of relief breathed from Reuben's mouth as he trotted down the steps to his bike. A big smile lit his face as he told Dad, 'It's okay. Everything's all right now.'

'Lose any fingers?' Dad joked as they turned into their own street.

'Nah,' Reuben replied. 'Actually, the dog's pretty friendly; he's just got a fierce bark.'

'That's the secret,' Dad said. 'Facing your fears and admitting your faults is the only way to overcome them. And you'll never have peace inside until you confess the sin that is weighing you down.'

'I know, Dad,' Reuben said. '*Now*, I know.' He grinned and pedalled faster. At last he wasn't afraid to face tomorrow.

28: FOLLOW THE STAR

> *For he that cometh to God must believe that he is, and that he is a rewarder of them that diligently seek him.*
> Hebrews 11:6

'Now when Jesus was born in Bethlehem of Judaea in the days of Herod the king, behold, there came wise men from the East to Jerusalem, saying, "Where is he that is born King of the Jews? For we have seen his star in the East, and are come to worship him."'

Have you ever looked up on a cold winter night and saw the bright specks of white scattered across the black sky? The longer you gazed, the more stars you saw. You may have noticed that some of the stars are brighter than others and some seem to form a shape. By going from dot to dot, you could even draw a picture with the stars!

There are people that study the stars; they are called astronomers. Astronomers have been studying the stars for thousands of years. During the time of the Israelite kings, many countries around Israel studied the stars to try to prophesy what was going to happen in their kingdom or in the world. At that time the people that studied the stars were often called wise men, or sorcerers and magicians. You have heard of them before, haven't you? Then listen now to a story about some wise men who were studying the night skies.

Far to the east of Israel, across deserts and mountains, was a foreign kingdom. In this kingdom there lived wise men. These men studied all kinds of things, from the skies and stars to the earth below. They knew the histories of the countries around them, and so they knew also about Israel. They knew how the Israelites had conquered Jericho and then the rest of Canaan. And they knew that the Israelites worshipped Jehovah, the unseen powerful God, not an image made by human hands.

These wise men also probably knew how Baalim, a prophet from their eastern kingdoms was once sent to curse Israel. But instead of cursing Israel, he blessed it, saying, 'I shall see him, but not now: I shall behold him, but not nigh: there shall come a Star out of Jacob, and a Sceptre shall rise out of Israel' (*Num.* 24:17). Baalim was prophesying of a star that would appear and a King that would then come from Israel.

And so one night, as these wise men were watching the night skies, tracing out the familiar movement and patterns of the stars, they suddenly saw a new star, a special star, the Star prophesied by Baalim many years ago.

'It is the Star of Jacob!' they must have told one another, 'the sceptre that would rise out of Israel is here! Their great King is born at last. Let us go and honour this King of kings.' And so they took rich gifts, prepared food, and readied their camels for the long journey.

For days they travelled through the desert, guided at night by the Star. And at last they reached Israel, the country of the new King. They must have hurried as they made their way to Jerusalem, the capital city, for soon they would see him, the one they had travelled so far to honour. To Jerusalem? Why did they travel to Jerusalem? Well, a king belongs to royalty, doesn't he? And royalty lives in a palace in the capital city, of course.

And so the wise men made their way to the palace in Jerusalem. They were a strange-looking procession of richly dressed men and heavily loaded camels. The people of Jerusalem must have stopped to stare, but when the wise men asked about the great King that had been born, they were met with puzzled looks and frowns. No one knew about him. They already had a king. An Edomite named Herod, set over them by the Romans. No, this was certainly not the King that the wise men were looking for.

Soon the wise men arrived at the palace. There King Herod asked them carefully about who they were looking for. He did not know where to send them, but asked the Israelite chief priests and scribes. They had an answer for the wise men. 'It says in the prophecy of Micah,' they tell the wise men, 'that the great Ruler shall be born in Bethlehem.'

The wise men then left King Herod, the palace, and Jerusalem. Once again the Star which they had first seen in their country appeared to lead them to Bethlehem. In Bethlehem, the star stopped over the place where Jesus was living. The wise men must have wondered about the small, plain house; this was no palace of a king. But in faith they entered and found Mary with the young child Jesus.

Then we read in the Bible that they fell down and worshipped Him. It was not King Herod, dressed in kingly robes, that they worshipped, but the King of all, this small child Jesus.

The wise men believed that this poor young boy living in a small house in Bethlehem was a King, and by faith they knew that He was to be worshipped as God. They opened their packs and gave to Him their kingly gifts of gold, frankincense, and myrrh.

The wise men travelled far, believing that they would find their King at the end of the journey. We do not need to travel far to find the Lord Jesus in Bethlehem, but instead, each Christmas time again, the Lord Jesus is brought to us in the Christmas stories, the Christmas songs, and the Christmas sermons. And like the wise men, we must believe in the Lord Jesus and seek Him, then rejoice in Him and worship Him when we find Him.

29: ONE SNOWY NIGHT

> *And you hath he quickened,*
> *who were dead in trespasses and sins.*
> Ephesians 2:1

Mary and Jeff, the note read. *Dad cut his finger. Had to take him to the emergency room – dropped Julia off at the Shermans.* Esther reached up and peeled the note off her grandparents' front door. Turning it to the light of a street lamp, she read the note again. *The Shermans?* she thought in surprise. Julia was supposed to be spending the afternoon at Grandma and Grandpa's while Mom and Dad were away for the day. What should she do? Mom had told her to walk over and pick up her sister at five o'clock, so they would both be home when Mom and Dad arrived after supper. But now Julia was at the Shermans, probably playing with their little girl.

Esther knew where the Shermans lived, but it was quite a long walk and it was growing dark out. Still, Mom and Dad wouldn't be back for at least an hour yet. Should she go back home and ask her older brother what to do? Wait, she knew what she could do. She would cut across the back pasture and through the apple orchard. Then she would come out on the Shermans' street, just a few houses down. She and Julia had gone that way once last summer. It would be much quicker than going all the way down the main street and up the Shermans' road.

Turning back the way she had come, Esther hurried down the sidewalk, stuffing the note into her pocket as she went. Nearing home, she turned off into a dead-end street. The end of it opened into a pasture, and beyond that lay the apple orchard. Climbing the wooden fence, Esther tramped down the sloping field.

It all looked so different from the summertime. Then the long grasses had scratched their bare legs. Now only the tips of summer's grass poked out from the blanket of snow. Then bright sky overhead and the smell of warm earth had made the walk a pleasant one. In the orchard, the shade from the apple trees had given relief from the hot sun. But now the last glow from the sun had disappeared, and the pale blue sky was quickly darkening. A thin sliver of moon had already risen high in the sky. It felt much later than five o'clock. Or was it five-thirty already?

Esther shivered. It seemed the sinking sun had drawn all the warmth from her with its descent behind the trees. She quickened her steps through the snow, her boots leaving a trail of deep footprints. Climbing the fence at the other end of the pasture, she followed the frozen creek up to the orchard, and crossed the wooden bridge. From there the way was clear.

Long rows of trees shoved bare branches against the sky. Here the snow was even deeper, but Esther paid no heed to it. Anxiously she hurried on, following the row of trees. The way was longer than she remembered from the summer. Then she and Julia had stopped and played along the way, but now she had to hurry and bring Julia back before Mom and Dad arrived home and wondered where they were.

At last she could see the end of the row. Eight more trees, six, three, one . . . there. Now, out on to the street. Here the going was much easier. A snowplough had come by and cleared the road of snow.

In a moment Esther was ringing the Shermans' doorbell. Mr and Mrs Sherman weren't home, but their oldest daughter helped bundle Julia into her coat and hat. 'It's cold out there, isn't it?' she asked while pulling Julia's scarf up over her nose. 'Here, let me tuck your mittens under your coat sleeves.'

Thanking her, Esther took Julia by the hand. The two girls stepped out from the front door, leaving the warm circle of light. Hurrying together down the driveway, they passed the neighbour's house.

'Here, we'll go through the orchard,' Esther told her sister as the rough branches came into view. Leaving the cleared road and the light from the streetlamps, they slid down the deep ditch and headed into the dim orchard. Now they had to walk more slowly, for Julia's short legs couldn't keep up with Esther's longer strides. Still, Julia lifted her feet high and trudged bravely along, stepping in Esther's footprints whenever she could.

The snow was much deeper here under the trees. Wide drifts formed blankets between the rows. It was too dark now to find the row she had come through, so Esther had to break a new trail. What fun she and Julia would have had throwing themselves into the drifts if the sun had still been up. How they would have laughed as they formed couches and tables out of the snow, building themselves a play-house. But the sun wasn't up, and instead of inviting them to make featherbeds, the drifts pulled at their boots, weighing each step down.

It was Esther who slowed the pace first. Her hurried walk over to the Shermans' had tired her.

'How are you doing, Julia?' she called back behind her.

'I'm okay,' the little voice chimed out brightly.

On and on they trudged, more and more slowly. Clouds drifted in front of the moon taking the dim glow from the snow below. The way through the orchard became a dark tunnel with trees pressing in on either side. Esther became uneasy, but even as her brain told her to hurry, her feet protested. Her toes seemed to burn, and her boots felt too tight. She tried to open her mouth to speak, but her lips felt thick, as though she'd been to the dentist for a freezing.

'How are you doing, Julia?' she mumbled.

'I'm okay,' the little voice called out bravely.

And then a small mitten tugged on her sleeve, pulling her hand from her pocket. 'You sound funny, Esther,' Julia said.

'I'm okay,' Esther murmured as the dark line of the creek came into view. 'We're almost home.'

It was quiet again as they each put their strength into pushing through the deep snow. Now Julia walked beside Esther, clinging to her hand. Quit staring at me, Esther wanted to say, but she was too tired. She could hardly seem to keep her eyes open. Head down, she plodded on and on. It seemed they had been following the creek for hours.

'When are we going to cross the bridge?' Julia's voice shook Esther out of her drowsy state.

Yes, when? Esther wondered in surprise. Where was the wooden bridge? Think! Esther told herself, for a thick fog seemed to fill her brain. 'Um . . .' she said aloud. 'Up there is Carson's pond.' She stopped and looked around. 'We must have gone too far. Come,' she added turning back.

Julia took her hand again as they turned back, and in a few minutes they could make out the dark outline of the bridge against the ice below. In a moment they were across and headed to the pasture. The snow seemed to grow deeper and deeper as their legs grew more tired.

'My feet are getting very cold,' Julia told Esther.

'Mm-hmmm,' Esther answered. It was funny, but her feet didn't feel cold anymore. In fact the cold didn't seem to bother her at all anymore. She paused a moment with Julia at the pasture fence. It looked so high that she wondered how she had ever climbed it on the way to the Shermans.

'Here, let's just rest a minute,' she mumbled, and sank down into the snow.

'But my feet are so cold,' Julia said. 'Can't we just hurry home, Esther?'

But Esther gave no answer. Ah, this felt much better. Her eyes slid shut as she relaxed. If she could just sit here for a few minutes, she would have new energy to hurry home. She should tell Julia that. Just a few minutes, she should say, but somehow . . . somehow . . . she couldn't . . . quite . . . find the words . . .

'Esther! Wake up!' Julia was shaking her.

Esther startled awake, then slid back into her comfortable position.

'Esther!' Julia's voice was urgent. 'Esther! Come on! Don't be silly. I know you're foolin' me, but we have to go home now!'

Strange, it sounded like Julia was crying. Silly girl. Didn't Julia know she just needed a moment's rest?

'Ow!' suddenly Esther jolted awake. Her eyes flew open to see Julia's face in front of hers.

'Stop that!' she demanded as the sharp little nails pinched her face again.

'You stop it!' Julia said and sniffed back her tears angrily. 'You stop that foolin', Esther, and get up right now.'

'I'm coming, I'm coming,' Esther said getting to her feet. Had she really fallen asleep? she wondered. Out here in the cold and dark? 'Hurry now,' she said and grabbed Julia's hand.

The way up the pasture was long and difficult, but the two girls helped each other on. At the top, with no strength left, they crawled under the fence. Then stumbling down the dead-end street, they turned on to their road. There, in the distance, gleamed the light from their front porch. Oh, how warm and inviting it looked!

New energy filled their trembling legs, and faster and faster they walked. At last they staggered up the front steps. Pushing open the door, they tumbled in.

Mom was there in an instant. 'Girls! Where were you?' she cried while pulling off their hats and scarves and coats. 'Dad's driving all over town looking for you, and I've been calling everyone I could think of.'

In stammering words, through frozen lips, the story came out. How Grandma and Grandpa suddenly had to go to the hospital. How Esther had found the note and gone to get Julia herself. How they had grown so cold and tired on the way back. And how Esther had fallen asleep in the snow.

'Oh, my girls,' Mom said and gathered them both in her arms. Her voice was thick with tears. 'We could have lost you both. I am so glad you are safe. Surely the Lord kept you safe. He gave Julia the strength to wake you.'

'I was so scared, Mommy,' Julia murmured against Mom's cheek. 'I kept calling Esther and shaking her, but she wouldn't wake up. Finally I was pinching and pinching her face.'

'You did right,' Mom assured her and hugged both girls close to her. 'Come, let's get some warm food in you and get you into your pyjamas. I'll call Dad on his cell phone.'

That night the girls cuddled close on either side of Dad as he read them a Bible story before bed.

'Why did the Lord Jesus raise that man from the dead?' Julia asked when Dad closed the story Bible.

'The Lord Jesus was showing His power,' Dad told the girls. 'He still raises people from the dead today. Did you know that? Not people's dead bodies, but their dead souls.'

Dad looked down at Esther. He could still see the red welts on her face where Julia had pinched her. 'You know how Esther had fallen asleep in the snow and couldn't wake up?' he asked. 'That's how we are: not only soundly sleeping, but dead in sins. And just like Esther needed someone else to wake her, we need the Lord Jesus to wake us from the dead and give us new life.'

'I don't feel dead,' Julia said. 'Even in my soul.'

'Then you need to ask the Lord Jesus to show you your sins,' Dad said gently. 'When you see your sin, you will pray urgently for Him to give you new life. And do you think He will?'

Julia nodded.

'He surely will,' Dad agreed. 'For after all, isn't that why He came to this earth as a baby? To awaken dead sinners like you and me.'

Esther smiled. 'And that's why we remember the Lord Jesus' birth at Christmas!' she said. 'He brought new life.'

30: A TALE OF AN UNGRATEFUL PUPPY

> *O give thanks unto the Lord;*
> *for he is good.*
> Psalm 136:1

'Look, Tom! Look!' Pauline called excitedly from the window.

'What?' Tom asked in a bored voice. His sister was always calling for him to come look at things.

'Come quick!' Pauline cried as a truck door slammed outside. 'Dad's got a puppy with him!' She dashed out of the door to meet Dad.

'A what?' Tom called after her. Had she said puppy? He threw down the Lego airplane he was working on and ran to the back door. Sure enough, into the laundry room came Dad with a dirty pup wriggling in his arms.

'Where did he come from? Whose is that? Is he for us? He's so dirty!' Pauline and Tom both spoke at once.

'Found him nosing along the creek in the back field. Don't rightly know where he's from,' Dad answered. 'Could be he's one of Jefferson's pups; his dog had a litter a while back. I'll give him a call and find out.' Dad tucked the pup under one arm and shrugged off his coat.

'Couldn't rightly leave the little feller out there. Here, Tom, why don't you see what a rag and a little warm water can do to clean him up.'

Dad handed the wriggling pup to Tom and headed for the kitchen to phone Jefferson. Pauline began filling a low bucket with warm water. 'He might not like this, Tom,' she warned, as Tom lowered the struggling pup into the water. And he didn't! As soon as the puppy touched the water, he began to leap and squirm, sending water all over the floor and drenching Tom's legs.

'Sit still, you wildcat!' Tom begged through clenched teeth. 'You're making a mess!' He held tightly to the warm, lively body, now dripping wet, as Pauline sloshed a wet rag over his dirt-matted fur.

'There, you're almost clean.' Pauline had just said this when with a sudden twist and jump the pup escaped Tom's hands and leaped out of the bucket. Like a mad thing he tore around and around the laundry room, tumbling over the shoe rack, skidding through the dirty laundry, and sending water everywhere. Pauline and Tom jumped out of his way and rescued the bucket of water from his path.

At last the pup stopped and stood trembling and panting by the door. Just then Dad returned. He looked at the mess: shoes everywhere, laundry everywhere, water everywhere.

At last he said, 'It's one of Jefferson's pups, all right. We can keep him if we want. This pup kept running away on him and at last he gave up on him.'

Dad looked at Tom's dripping clothes. 'You sure you want him, Tom and Pauline?' he asked.

'I don't think he wants us,' Pauline said doubtfully.

'But I want him,' Tom answered. 'We'll keep him.'

Later that afternoon Tom fed the pup a little dog food. He was so hungry that he gobbled up the food in moments. But when Tom reached for the bowl to fill it again, the little pup growled at him and tried to nip his hand. Frustrated, Tom got another bowl and filled it with more dog food before setting it down. Hungrily the little pup ate all that too, then lapping up some water from his bowl, turned his back on Tom and lay down near the door.

After supper Tom went over to the puppy and tried to coax him up to play with a rubber ball. The pup showed no interest, however, and showed his little white teeth in a growl when Tom tried to pet him.

That night Tom went to bed feeling disappointed. He had done everything he could think of to make the puppy happy. Before turning off Tom's light, Dad came in and sat on his bed.

'He's not a very friendly little guy, is he?' Dad said referring to the puppy.

'I guess not,' Tom said. 'But why's he got to be so mean? I gave him food and water, and we cleaned him, and I only wanted to play with him, and all he does is growl at me and try to bite me. What's the point of being nice? How would he have liked it if we just left him at the creek instead of taking care of him? It's not fair. I wanted a pup so bad, and we're taking good care of him, and he don't even like me!'

'That does seem hard,' Dad agreed. 'Still, I think your pup is just a little scared. He's been hungry and alone out there, and everything's new to him. Give him a few days. He'll come around. Soon you won't know what you ever did without him!' Dad got up to close the curtains.

'I hope so,' Tom sighed, ''cause I sure don't like it. When you're nice to someone, you expect them to be nice back.'

'Yeah, I know what you mean,' Dad said sitting back down on the bed. 'When we're kind to someone, we expect them to be kind and thankful back to us. And it hurts if they won't be. But it reminds me of what we read tonight at suppertime: the story of the servant that owed his master lots of money. Remember how he was going to be taken to jail, but he begged his master to give him more time to pay the money?'

'Yeah,' said Tom, 'and then his master forgave him, and he didn't have to pay any of the money.'

'That's right,' Dad said. 'So you would think that now he would be thankful and kind to other people. But what did he go and do instead?'

Tom thought a moment. 'He went and found another servant that owed him money, and said if he didn't pay right away, he'd throw him in jail. He was a mean guy. Is that what you meant about the puppy? That we were nice to him, and he's just mean back to us?'

'Yeah, that does sound like the puppy right now,' Dad said, 'but I was thinking more that we often act like that too. We're so disappointed when someone's unthankful to us, but we do it all the time to God. God gives us so many good things, and we don't show any thankfulness back.'

Dad stood and pulled the covers up over Tom. 'How do you figure we can thank God for His blessings?'

'We can tell Him we're thankful when we pray,' Tom said.

'That's right,' Dad said stopping in the doorway. 'Good-night, Tom. Before you turn out that light, why don't you look up Psalm 66 and see what else we should do when God's been so good to us?' ♧

31: SUMMER VACATION

> *The judgments of the LORD are true . . .*
> *in keeping of them there is great reward.*
> Psalm 19:9, 11

FRIDAY, JUNE 23

It is the last day of school and the air is filled with excited chatter. 'No more pencils! No more books! No more school bags on our hooks . . . !' rings out on the big yellow school bus as it slowly pulls out of the school driveway. 'Time for summer! Time for fun! Time for playing in the sun!' You are almost bouncing in your seat from excitement. Two whole months of free time. No more homework. No more getting up early in the morning. Summer vacation! You can hardly wait.

MONDAY, JUNE 26

You bounce out of bed. No school! Is the first thought that comes into your mind. What am I going to do first today? There's so much to do, I can hardly choose! Go biking, go to the park, fly my new kite, go swimming in my neighbours' pool if they're home . . . I've got loads of time to work on painting a picture without Mom calling, 'Time for bed!'

Maybe I'll build a tree fort, or make a bow and arrow. I'll have time to teach my dog some new tricks, and if it gets hot, I can set up a lemonade stand and get rich! Then I'll have to decide what to do with all my money. Maybe I'll use it to buy a pair of rollerblades.

Without wasting another minute, you pull on some shorts and a tee-shirt, and you're ready to go.

WEDNESDAY, JULY 5

A week and a half has passed, and you're sitting on the kitchen counter swinging your legs. Mom is getting lunch ready.

'Mom, I'm bored,' you announce. 'There's nothing to do.'

'School has only been out for a week,' Mom answers, 'and you're bored already? What are you going to do when August comes?'

'I don't know. There's nothing to do.'

'Well,' Mom thinks for a moment, 'why don't you take your little sister out and play hopscotch until lunch; she has been asking you all morning. And after lunch you could go biking, or get in some soccer practice, or build a town in the sandbox with your brother.'

'It's too hot outside,' you complain. 'When will the neighbours be back, so we can go swimming again?'

'Next week, I think,' Mom replies. 'You were saying yesterday that you can't find any of your art supplies; you could clean out your desk and organize all your supplies. Then when you want to paint, everything will be ready . . . Or how about that new book you got for your birthday? It looked pretty exciting.'

'Can't I have a friend over?' you ask.

'Next week you may,' Mom answers. 'And in the meantime, your brother and sister would love it if you played with them. Now how about some hopscotch?'

With a sigh, you hop down off the counter and go out to find your sister.

ஃ

Summer vacation. How do you spend it? Or maybe a better question is: how *should* you spend it? We can find the answer to that in the Bible.

'We can?' you ask in surprise. Yes, for even though the Bible does not give us a list of things to do and things not to do during our summer vacation, the Bible does teach us about the heart attitude we must have. And the first place we can look in the Bible is at the ten commandments found in Exodus 20. God gave these laws to Moses to read to the Israelites, and these laws are still here for us to obey today.

Let's look at the fifth commandment. It says, 'Honour thy father and mother.' What does that mean? And what does that have to do with summer vacation?

Well, imagine that you are bored, and you go to your mom. When you complain that there's nothing to do, she gives you a suggestion. How do you react? Do you say, 'Oh, that's boring too; I don't feel like doing that.' Or, 'It's too hot, and I'm too tired; I want to do something different'? When you respond like that, are you honouring your mother? Not at all. Next time that you ask for something to do, go out cheerfully and try what she suggests. And remember, an unhappy spirit takes all the joy out of things. So go happily, and using all the imagination and creativity that God has given you, enjoy it.

Now imagine you are just building a tree fort when your dad asks you to help with some work in the yard. What response will honour your father? When you go with a cheerful heart, willingly, not dragging your feet. And while you're helping, enjoy the time you spend with your dad. Ask him questions about the work you're doing. Ask why certain things need to be done in the yard and how they need to be done. Watch and learn how to help your dad in his work. You'll be surprised to find that the more effort you put in, the more you enjoy the work!

Turn with me now to the fourth commandment. There we read, 'Remember the Sabbath day, to keep it holy.' This commandment also teaches us something about how we spend our summer vacation. When God created the world, He worked for six days and rested on the seventh day. He tells us to do this too. From Monday to Saturday we can work and play, but Sunday is a special day, a rest day, a day to keep separate from the rest of the week.

This means that we spend Sundays differently from other days; instead of being busy with our work and play, we are busy with God's work and worship. So this commandment teaches us that on Sundays during your summer vacation, you need to rest from your work and instead do things that will help you learn about God.

The last commandment that we will look at today was not given in the ten commandments, but was given by the Lord Jesus. In Matthew 20, Jesus was talking to the Pharisees about the ten commandments. He told them that the greatest commandment was to 'love the Lord thy God with all thy heart, and with all thy soul, and with all thy mind', and then to 'love thy neighbour as thyself'.

And what does this have to do with spending your summer vacation? Loving your neighbour as yourself means thinking of what someone else would like to do, instead of always doing what you want. Instead of thinking, 'I'm bored, and I have nothing to do, and I want to do something fun', ask yourself: 'What would my sister like me to do with her? What would help my mom? What would my little brother want to play?' If you have this heart attitude of loving the Lord and loving your neighbour as yourself, you will find happiness, for in keeping God's commands there is great reward. 🐛

32: THE ABANDONED BASSOON

Have you heard the old story of a missing horseshoe nail?

A soldier was leading his horse back to camp when he realized that his horse was limping. Bending down, he examined the horse's hoof. Its horseshoe was loose; it was missing a nail. He would have to get that replaced immediately. Just then the call came for dinner. The soldier hesitated. He would replace the nail right after dinner, he decided. But the line of men waiting for food was long, and by the time the soldier had eaten, the sun had set. 'I'll get it done tomorrow before dinner,' he assured himself. And the next morning, the battle began again.

But because of the nail, the shoe was lost,

And because of the shoe, the horse was lost.

Because of the horse, the soldier was lost,

WAIT TILL YOU SEE THE BUTTERFLY

And because of the soldier, the battle was lost.

Because of the battle, the war was lost.

All because of a missing nail.

Our actions have consequences, don't they? One act of kindness can lead to many other acts of kindness, and one act of sin can lead to many other sins.

Brap, breep, braump!

'Oh, I'm never gonna be able to learn this song.' Matt put down the bassoon in disgust. 'It's way too hard! Anyways,' he continued. 'I've already been practising for at least ten minutes. Where's my book?'

And with that he flopped on to his bed with an adventure book. Within moments he was lost with his hero in the jungles of Brazil.

'Matt!' Mom called down the stairs five minutes later. 'Are you practising your bassoon?'

'Uh, yeah, sort of,' his voice trailed off. 'I already did,' he excused himself under his breath. He stretched and rolled over to get more comfortable.

The next school day found Matt sitting in band practice.

'Bassoons, can I hear that line again? Right on the second entrance.' The band director dropped his hand and the two bassoons played their line. Well, one of them actually played. Matt only made a few hesitant squawks.

Mr Meyer stopped the two of them. 'Hmm,' he said. 'Matt, same line as last Tuesday. You said you were going to work on it at home.'

Matt blew out his breath in frustration. 'I couldn't,' he mumbled. 'I've had a bad cough.'

'All right,' Mr. Meyer said. 'Then give it some work in the next few days, please.'

Matt picked up his bassoon with a little cough. He tried to follow along for the rest of the practice, but he had lost his concentration. You don't have a bad cough, his conscience declared loudly in his head. You were just too lazy to practice.

That night Matt was lying on his bed with the second book in his adventure series. His bassoon sat untouched in its case. 'Matt,' Dad's voice sounded from the doorway. 'Put the book away; you've got to practise. You wanted to play the bassoon, we bought you one, and now you have to keep your end of the deal: fifteen minutes a day.'

Matt sighed, rolled over, and dropped his book on the floor. He took out his bassoon and quickly ran through his music pieces. That same line was as tricky as ever. He hadn't paid much attention last band practice, and now he couldn't get the rhythm. Matt quickly grew discouraged and put the instrument away after only five minutes of practice.

'All done, Matt?' Mom asked as she passed his room a little later.

'Yup,' he answered without even looking up. This time he hardly even heard his conscience.

Next Tuesday at band practice, the director asked to hear the same line from the bassoons. Matt hunched his shoulders, brought his bassoon to his mouth and, like the last two practices, muddled his way through it. He was relieved when Mr Meyer didn't say anything about his poor rhythm, but went on to the next piece of music. Mr Meyer stopped Matt on his way out of practice, however.

'What's going on, Matt?' he asked him in a kind voice. 'You were doing so well at the beginning of the year, and now it just doesn't seem like you're putting in any practice time at home.'

Matt felt his face grow red. That's right, his conscience announced. Admit it. You just haven't felt like practising. Tell him you'll do better this week. But Matt opened his mouth and stammered. 'Well, really, I haven't been able to practice. I still have this bad cough and my mom said I shouldn't overdo it.' And he gave a small cough.

Mr Meyer looked at Matt for a moment, and finally said, 'Well, let's get that cold over with quickly, so you can get back into it again.'

Matt gave a nod and hurried off, pushing away the voice of his conscience.

That Thursday, Matt slipped off to the library when it was time for band practice. His cousin Philip had come over last night, and Matt's parents hadn't noticed that he hadn't touched his bassoon. He dared not face Mr Meyer, so he would use band practice time to do some homework he had also not gotten to last night.

Later that day, Matt passed Mr Meyer in the hallway. The band director looked surprised to see him. 'I didn't see you in practice today,' he said.

'Yeah, uh, I need to take some time off to get over this cold,' Matt lied easily.

'But you were cutting class," Mr. Meyers said pointedly.

'Yeah, uh, I had a note from my mom,' Matt reached into his pocket and pretended to search for the note. 'Uh, I don't know where it went.'

Mr Meyer looked Matt in the eyes. Finally he said, 'Very well, bring the note in tomorrow. We're performing in two weeks, but unless you are able to practise, I don't think you'll be ready to join us.'

The next afternoon, Matt was heading to his locker with a piece of notebook paper gripped tightly in his sweaty hand. He had been avoiding Mr Meyer all day, but now as he saw him walking by, he quickly passed him the note.

'How are you, Matt,' Mr. Meyer greeted him, and to Matt's dismay, he stopped right there and opened the note. Scanning the note quickly, he looked for a moment at the signature at the bottom. 'From your mom?' he asked Matt.

Matt didn't give his conscience a chance to speak, but quickly nodded his head and turned to his locker. When he looked up, the band director was gone.

That night at the dinner table, Matt was sullen and quiet. He gave a short answer when his mom asked how his day was at school. He snapped at his sister when she asked for help on her project, and he mumbled an 'all right' when his dad asked how band practice was going.

'I can't wait till I get to play in the band,' Matt's younger brother said.

'Well, you just watch the band at their performance next week and see which instrument you like best,' his mom told him.

Matt glared down at his plate. Would everyone please stop talking about the band? he thought angrily.

Just then the phone rang. Dad got up to answer it. 'Mr Meyer,' he said in his friendly voice. 'What can I do for you?'

Matt gulped and felt his face turn pale. Now he was caught. It would all come out – how he hadn't practised at home, how he had lied to his parents, how he had lied to the band director, how he had cut class, and how he had forged his mom's signature. He knew he was in deep trouble.

'Did you think this would be worth it?' his conscience asked. This time there was no quieting the voice. 'You thought one little lie was no big deal? Now look at what you've done! You've ruined your relationship with your parents and your teacher, you've been a bad example to your brothers and sisters, no one can trust you anymore, and you've sinned against the Lord.'

Biting his lower lip, Matt waited anxiously for Dad to hang up the phone. 🐌

33: THE INVITATION

> *Ask, and it shall be given you;*
> *Seek, and ye shall find;*
> *Knock, and it shall be opened unto you.*
> Matthew 7:7

A large group of people stand gathered at the door of a great stone castle. Their feet shuffle on the ground raising dust, just as their voices are raised to be heard over all the noise. Young and old are gathered there; women and children are seen among the men and the grey-headed. They have come from far, from all over the countryside. What has brought them here?

A stranger has visited their country, and told them of a great Prince who has invited them to his castle. The stranger also told them the way to the castle. And the people? What did they do with the stranger's message? Many of them went to find out if his invitation was true, but many more stayed home; they were too busy, tired, lazy, or didn't believe his message. But the people who listened began the journey to the castle. In each mind was the question: what will I have to do to be allowed in to see the Prince?

And so here is this great commotion of people, gathered before the door of the Prince's castle. They seem to be arguing. Come closer, and you can hear what they are saying. Listen to the group of men standing closest to the heavy iron door.

'How can that be?' one man asks, pointing up to some words carved in stone above the great door.

Look up, and you can read the words too.

KNOCK AND THE DOOR SHALL BE OPENED UNTO YOU.

'Why would the Prince open the door if we knocked?' the man asks. 'We're only peasants – the poor people from our country.'

'That's right,' his neighbour agrees. 'Besides, how could the Prince even hear us? He's probably busy inside.'

A few feet away stand some mothers busy with their children. 'I'm hot, Mother,' a little boy complains. 'May we leave soon?'

'Hush, child,' his mother replies. 'Soon. Father said it is important that we come, but soon we can leave.'

A small baby starts to cry, and its mother bounces it gently, trying to calm her child. The father is looking thoughtfully up at the words above the door.

KNOCK AND THE DOOR SHALL BE OPENED UNTO YOU.

'Hmm,' he says to himself. 'So there really is a castle, and we really do have a Prince. It's good to know that. Maybe we'll come back some day when we have more time. Come along, children,' he calls, and his family follows him down the path, away from the castle.

The Invitation

An old man and woman slowly edge their way through the crowd up to the great doors. With dim eyes they carefully make out the words carved in the stone. 'Knock!' the old man says surprised. 'Is that all, wife? There must be some mistake. It cannot be so easy.' Helpfully he tucks his wife's arm through his, and arm in arm they shuffle away.

'Besides,' he adds with one last look at the castle, 'what would we do in the castle anyways? We're old. It's better for us to go back to our home.'

A group of boys are standing to the side of the door, talking about the words. 'You go,' one boy says pushing his friend. 'You go first, then we'll follow.'

'I'm not going,' he protests. 'Everyone's watching. No way.'

'Look!' another of the boys exclaims. 'There's some trees growing up against the castle wall. Let's see if we can climb them and get over the wall!'

'You won't make it,' the first boy replies. 'They're not tall enough.'

'Who cares! Let's just try it,' his friend answers, and off they scamper to the trees.

Suddenly a man comes forward out of the crowd. The people step aside to let him through. He is dressed more neatly than the other poor peasants. He walks boldly up to the doors, frowns up at the words, then putting both hands to the door handle, pulls at the great door. But nothing happens.

'Pah!' the man scowls and spits in the dirt. In injured pride he turns and hurries away down the path.

Over to the side we can see two other men, busy with a piece of iron. They are prying at the hinges, seeing if the door can be opened that way. But they too, cannot force the door open.

Coming up along the side of the crowd is a young man and woman. They have carefully prepared themselves to meet the Prince. You can see that their hair and clothing is neat, in their hand is a gift for the Prince, and they have prepared a beautiful speech to read to the Prince.

'Where is the servant that keeps the door?' the young man asks when he gets to the door.

'I don't see any servant,' the young woman answers him. 'It says we must knock.'

'What? No servants?' the young man exclaims in disgust. 'What kind of a Prince and castle is this? Let us leave this place at once.' And with that, he and the young woman turn away.

And so it goes on. Some are curious about the words, some wonder if they are really true. Some are in too much of a hurry to stay long. Some wonder if there is a way to get in without knocking. Some are trying to make themselves ready to see the Prince. And some are too embarrassed to go forward and knock.

Then the sky grows dark. Heavy grey clouds cover the sun. Rain begins to fall, first in drops, and then in great sheets of water. The people try to shield their faces from the rain. Many peasants, bothered by the rain and disappointed with the words they saw above the gate, turn away and hurry back down the path to find shelter.

But do they all leave? No, a few stay behind, squinting longingly up at the words carved in stone. We will stay also, for look! Over there. A small figure comes hurrying up the path. It is a young girl, her clothes soaked through by the rain, and water streaming out of her shoes.

'Am I too late?' she asks, out of breath. But no one answers. They turn and look silently from the words down to the girl. 'What is it?' she asks once more. 'Will the Prince not let us in after all? What must we do to come to him?'

In answer, an old man points slowly up at the words carved above the door.

KNOCK AND THE DOOR SHALL BE OPENED UNTO YOU.

'Is that the way?' the girl cries. 'Then I am not too late after all!' And with that she hurries to the great door, raises her small white hand and knocks. The others look in wonder as the great door to the castle swings open and then closes as the girl disappears inside.

§⚘

Jesus spoke these words about coming to Him, the Prince of Peace: 'Knock and it shall be opened unto you.' He also said, 'Seek and ye shall find; ask and it shall be given unto you.' What has been your response? ⚘

34: A VALUABLE ACCIDENT

> *Hear, O LORD, when I cry with my voice:*
> *have mercy also upon me, and answer me.*
> Psalm 27:7

The church service was coming to an end. Alex stood up with his family as the congregation rose to sing the last Psalm. He waited quietly as the elder of the church filed out, but his mind was busy. The minister's last question still rang through his head.

The minister had preached on the story of blind Bartimaeus. Alex had already heard that story a few years ago in Sunday school and in family Bible reading, but he had never thought that it had much to do with him. Today, however, the minister had asked the congregation if they cried out to Jesus like blind Bartimaeus did. And now Alex was still thinking about that.

'Do I cry out to the Lord Jesus to have mercy on me?' Alex wondered as he started filing out of church. 'I always pray for forgiveness and for a new heart,' he thought, 'but I don't think I really cry out for it. And sometimes I even think that the Lord won't hear my prayer, so I just sort of pray without paying attention.'

Alex put his money in the collection plate and stepped out into the bright sunshine. He headed over to his cousins who were standing by the edge of the parking lot.

'Hey, Alex!' Carl called to him. 'Guess how many more hours till we leave for the cottage?'

Alex grinned at his cousin. All thoughts and questions about the sermon went right out of his head. Carl was his age and was just as excited about going up north as Alex was. Their families were leaving early tomorrow morning, and they would meet some more family up there.

'Um, twelve more hours?' he guessed.

'Close!' Carl answered. 'Eleven! We're leaving at five o'clock to beat the traffic.'

❦

The drive to the cottage was long, but at last the car left the highway and began winding its way down gravel roads. Excitement built within Alex as they followed the rocky shoreline dotted with pine trees. Within minutes, Dad slowed the van and turned into a long driveway.

'We're here!' Alex whooped sticking his head out of the car window.

Carl's family had arrived just ahead of them, and, already, Alex could see Carl running over to greet him.

'What do you want to do first?' he asked breathlessly.

'Whoa! Slow down; just a minute!' Dad interrupted. 'First we have some luggage to unload. Help with the duffel bags, Alex, then your Mom and I will get the rest.'

It took a few minutes to unload, but Alex had never worked faster. Carl helped him, and while the last bag was being brought to the cabin, he turned to run to the dock. 'I'll get the canoe ready,' he told Alex.

Alex tossed the last bag onto his bed, then headed out the door to the dock.

'Oh! One more thing, Alex,' Mom called after him. 'Could you bring these pies over to Mr Kirkland? He has the cottage just around the bend in the lake. They're still frozen, so I would like to get them to him before they thaw out.' At Alex's frown, Mom continued, 'He is such a nice man, and it's his first summer here alone since his wife died.'

'But Mom!' Alex protested, 'Carl's already gone to get the canoe out. I don't have time right now. Can't Cassie bring them?' At his mother's sigh, he added, 'I'll do it right when I get back.'

'Go, then,' Mom said and set the pies back down on the counter. Alex ran off toward the docks as Mom finished unpacking the coolers. She would bring the pies over herself.

The next few days were spent in canoeing, fishing, volley-ball, and swimming. The two boys couldn't get enough of being outside and running around together. Each day they wanted to do more than the day before. By the time Friday came, they should have been tired out, but instead, they were itching for still more adventure.

'I know,' Carl said as they loosened the canoe from the dock. 'Let's explore past the island, around the bend in the lake.'

'Nah,' Alex disagreed. 'It gets too choppy out there, and, besides, it'll be getting dark in an hour.'

'Well, where else will we go?' Carl protested. 'We've been down the creek three times and on the island ten times. Let's try it.' And with that, he stepped into the canoe and pushed off.

Twenty minutes of steady paddling brought the boys to the island. Another ten minutes and they were rounding the bend in the lake. Here the going became harder as the wind was against them, and the choppy waves pushed back their canoe.

'Come on!' Carl shouted over his shoulder. 'Head to that fallen tree on the shore, and we'll tie up there for a few minutes.'

The two boys paddled hard and soon reached the tree. Alex leaned over to tie the rope to one of the branches just as Carl stepped out on to a rock. The canoe jerked and Carl's foot slipped on the wet rock. With a cry, he fell backwards, scraping his back on the edge of the canoe and then hitting his head. He rolled over and tried to get up, but only slumped forward over the edge of the canoe. A spot of blood darkened his hair.

Quickly, Alex scrambled into the water to help him. 'Come on! Pull yourself in!' he encouraged.

Carl reached weakly with his arms for the seat and tugged himself another inch or two into the canoe. Then he groaned, 'I can't. My head. It's so dizzy.'

Clenching his teeth, Alex grabbed hold of Carl's legs and shoved him the rest of the way in. Then he looked at the water. It had gotten really choppy. He'd never be able to get the canoe back by himself. Alex felt panic and looked along the rocky shoreline for a spot to pull up the canoe.

Then he saw it. Mr Kirkland's cabin. Just beyond a stand of pine trees. Alex hesitated. The conversation in the kitchen with his mom came rushing back into his memory. 'He is such a nice man,' Mom had said, 'And it's his first summer here alone since his wife died.' Then he heard himself say, 'But Mom! . . . I don't have time right now.'

Shame filled him, but as he looked back at Carl lying helpless in the canoe, Alex knew what he had to do.

※

'It's a good thing you boys landed near my cabin,' Mr Kirkland said glancing back over his shoulder. 'A few hundred metres farther up the lake and you wouldn't have found help for miles.'

Carl was lying in the back seat of Mr Kirkland's car, and Alex was sitting up front. Mr. Kirkland had hurried down to help the boys when Alex had arrived white-faced at his cabin door, begging for help. Now Mr Kirkland was driving them home. They would have to come back for the canoe later.

Pulling up the driveway into the campground, Alex mustered up his courage to thank Mr. Kirkland.

'Thanks a lot,' he said. 'I mean, we never really deserved your help.'

Mr Kirkland put the car into park and glanced over with a question in his eyes.

'I mean,' Alex quickly explained, 'You're helping us, and we've never really done anything for you before.' And he told Mr Kirkland about the pies.

'That's all right, son,' Mr. Kirkland said leaning over to clap Alex on the shoulder. 'We sinners are often like that. We have no use for anyone else, even for our Lord, until we're in trouble. But then we start calling loudly enough for help!'

'Just like blind Bartimaeus!' Alex said in surprise. And Sunday's sermon came back to him: 'Jesus, thou son of David, have mercy on me.' Alex remembered how the sermon had made an impression on him. He had also meant to cry out to the Lord that night. He had meant to, but he had quickly forgotten his need.

But not this time! Alex said to himself as they were helping Carl out of the car. I must continue to pray and to cry to the Lord for forgiveness and a new heart. Jesus did hear blind Bartimaeus, and the minister said the Lord hears all sinners when they cry to Him. I won't give up praying and just hope that somehow the Lord will save me; I will be like Bartimaeus and cry all the more.

How do you pray to the Lord? Quickly and out of habit? Ask the Lord to show you your need. Then you will cry to Him urgently and continually like blind Bartimaeus. ❧

35: GOOD INTENTIONS

That ye might walk worthy of the Lord unto all pleasing, being fruitful in every good work, and increasing in the knowledge of God.
Colossians 1:10

'Please take out your journals, boys and girls,' Mrs. Robinson said. 'We are going to write a short piece about our summer vacations . . .'

A rustle and clatter was heard in the classroom as the children pulled out their journals and found a pencil to write with. Karen was having trouble finding her journal in her desk. She pushed aside a piece of crumpled paper and peered between each book. Aha! There it is. Now where's my pencil? She unzipped her pencil case. Nope, no pencil there. She felt around in the back of her desk. Yup, there's a pencil. Man! How did it get back there? And I was so sure that I was going to keep my desk neat this year! Already a mess, and it's only the first week of school.

The children's heads were bent over their books as they began writing. Travis was daydreaming, staring out the window.

'Travis,' Mrs. Robinson called him, 'You had better get started with the rest of the class.'

Travis's face turned red. This was the second time the teacher had called his name today, and he had told Mom that he would do better this year. No more daydreaming, he had said.

Sandra's pencil was flying across the page. She had so much to write about! The day when her cousins came over and they all played Capture the Flag, the time her dog ran away and they had to find him, and about switching bedrooms with her sister. She had just finished a whole page of writing and was ready to go on to the next page. She looked back at the page that she had written. Oh no! she groaned. My work is so messy! Why can't I write neater like all the other girls? I was sure that this year my work would stay neat. I guess I had better slow down on the next page.

&.

Does this sound familiar to you? Starting a new school year we all think things like: This year I'm going to be neater, this year I'm going to work harder, I'm going to be nicer to the other kids, I'll study more for tests . . . And on New Year's Eve, when we start a new year in January, we hear the same things.

'What's your New Year's resolution?' we ask each other.

'Oh, this year I'm going to learn to play the trumpet. I'm going to practise the piano more. Me? I'm going to do things right away; I'm not going to wait till the last minute anymore.' Or, 'This year I'm going to play with my dog every day. I won't argue with my brother anymore.'

We're full of good intentions, aren't we? Full of new plans and things we promise ourselves. 'I'm going to do this, I won't do this, I'll always do this' . . . our lists go on and on. And then before we know it, we've slipped back into our old habits again. Our desks have become a disaster zone, we haven't practised the piano in weeks, and we started our Science project the night before it was due.

'Oh well,' we might say. 'No one's perfect. Anyhow, it's no use trying. I can't change.'

Is it any use to make resolutions? Should we even bother?

Yes! It is good to try to do things well. We need goals and these resolutions we have mentioned are good.

Then how come we give up and quit so easily? How come within the first week of school, we're back to our old habits from last year? Is it because we don't try hard enough? Or could there be another reason? Could it be because we don't have the right motive?

The right motive? What's a motive?

A motive is our heart's attitude. It shows not just what we are doing, but also why we are doing it. And this is what the Lord looks at. Why are we trying to be nice to other kids? Because we want them to like us? Or because we really care about them? Why do we want our hand-writing to be neat? So that we will look like everyone else? So that we will be popular? Or simply to do our best in all our work and to please our teacher?

Think about playing the piano for a moment. Why do we want to play the piano well? To impress people? To please our parents who are paying for our lessons? Or so that others can enjoy our music. Couldn't we even want to play well in order to use the talents God gave us and to praise Him with our music?

You see, we can do something as simple as playing the piano, with good or bad motives!

So often we fail in our resolutions because we do not have good motives. First we need to have a good motive for what we are doing. Then, if we know our heart and actions will please God, we can pray as we work on our bad habit. And in this way we can succeed.

So the next time you say, 'From now on I'm going to . . .' first ask yourself, 'Why? Why do I want to be better at this? Do I want to please God?' And if you do want to please the Lord, then work at it! And ask for His help in prayer.

To end with, read Paul's prayer for the Colossians. You can make this your prayer and with God's help, your resolution.

'That ye might walk worthy of the Lord unto all pleasing,
being fruitful in every good work, and increasing in
the knowledge of God.'

COLOSSIANS 1:10

36: RASCAL

PART ONE

They had been sledding all morning at the neighbour's just across the road from their farm. Now they were coming home. Danny was dragging his snowboard behind him, and Rascal, his dog, was running ahead. He bounded joyfully over the drifts, his tail wagging happily as Danny threw snowballs for him to catch. They were almost at the neighbour's driveway. From there, they would race to the road where Rascal would wait panting for Danny to catch up.

'Race you to the road!' Danny shouted.

The dog stopped still in his tracks, waiting.

'Ready? Go!'

Like a shot, Rascal took off down the long driveway. His feet came together in a gallop like a horse, and his brown and white fur gleamed in the winter sun. Danny trotted behind, not even trying to keep up. At the end of the driveway, the dog skidded to a stop, then looked back panting, a long pink tongue hanging from the side of his mouth. He cocked his head as if to say, 'Well? Aren't you coming?'

Still waiting, he started sniffing around in the snow by the mailbox. Suddenly he raised his head and pricked his ears. A truck was coming. He knew the sound of that truck. It was Danny's Dad coming home in the old pickup. Sure enough, the truck appeared around the bend in the road, then slowed to turn into their driveway.

For just a second Rascal waited. He whined impatiently at the pickup, hesitated, and turned to look back at Danny. Finally, the truck fast disappearing up the driveway was too much for him. With a bound, he dashed over the road after the truck, eager to chase it to the barn, eager to welcome Danny's Dad home.

'Rascal!' Danny shouted. 'Wait!'

Just then a car came speeding around the bend. Too late the driver saw the dog crossing the road. Too late he swerved on to the shoulder of the road. He caught the dog with his bumper, then spun out of control and rolled the car into the ditch.

'NO! Rascal!' Danny screamed as the dog went somersaulting through the air. Danny tore down the driveway and across the road to where the dog had hit the side of the road. He fell to his knees and tried to help the dog to his feet. Rascal looked up at the boy with trusting brown eyes. He whimpered softly.

'Come on, boy,' Danny coaxed desperately through his tears. 'You'll be okay. Come on.' The dog struggled to get to his feet, but collapsed to the ground again, blood running from his side. 'No! You can't die! Rascal! Rascal!' Danny sobbed as he buried his face in the dog's neck. The dog shuddered, gave his last breath, and laid down his head on Danny's knees.

How long he sat there holding the dog, Danny didn't know. As if through a fog, he heard another car stop and the driver call the police. His dad, hearing all the commotion, came out to the road to see what had happened and what could be done. 'An ambulance is on its way', the other driver told him. At last Dad came over to Danny and tried to tug him to his feet, telling him that the dog was dead.

'No!' Danny cried and pulled away from Dad's comforting hand. Pressing his lips together to keep back another sob, he turned and ran down the long gravel driveway. His feet took him out to the back field – the field where he had spent so many happy hours with Rascal. His mind felt frozen. The thought pounded in his head that Rascal was dead. His lively, warm, friendly dog with the floppy ears and sloppy pink tongue . . . was dead. Lying still, on the side of the road. Danny could not believe it.

After lunch, Dad headed out to the back corner of the lawn, shovel in hand. Danny watched for a moment as Dad forced the shovel into the frozen earth to bury the dog, then turned away from the window. Going to his room, he sat on the edge of his bed. A few snowflakes drifted past his bedroom window. Danny got up to look out at the sky. It had grown grey with the promise of snow. He watched the flakes settle on the windowsill, each flake with a perfect design of its own. He wondered how long the snow would last. With a warm spell coming up, all the snow would likely melt.

The flakes fell thicker and faster now, blocking his view. Danny could hardly see his Dad across the lawn, putting the shovel away in the shed. He pressed his nose against the cold glass, his thoughts whirling like the snowflakes. Why even snow if it is just going to melt anyway? he wondered. And his thoughts went back to his dog.

Tears slipped down his cheeks as he leaned his forehead on the icy window. 'I don't get it,' Danny whispered to himself. 'Why can't the good things last? Why did Rascal have to die? Why does anything or anyone have to die?'

There was a faint click at the door, and Danny raised his head. Mom carefully opened the door, then came in. She sat down on the edge of Danny's bed. Her face looked sad too. She didn't say anything, but just looked at Danny.

Danny sniffed and walked over to sit on the bed next to her.

'He was the best dog in the world,' he said softly, and tears fell down his cheeks again. 'He was my very best friend.'

'I know,' Mom said putting her arm around Danny's shoulders. 'I know.'

'Then why did he have to die?' Danny asked more loudly. 'I'd rather never even have had a dog than have it hit by a car. Why did he have to die?'

Mom was gazing thoughtfully out the window. 'I don't know why, Danny, but I do know two things. The first is that nothing happens by chance. God is always in control, even when sad or bad things happen. He has a plan that is perfect. And the second thing is that God created this world as a perfect, beautiful, joyful place full of animals and plants and two people to take care of it. But you know how Adam and

Eve sinned and chose disobedience instead of life. Because we humans are their children and are born in sin, we too must die one day. So you see that it was people who brought death into the world."

'But Rascal never sinned, so why did he have to die?' Danny asked. 'It's doesn't seem fair. He never did anything wrong. Why did God let him die?'

'No,' Mom agreed still looking out into the snow-filled sky. 'Animals do not sin; they suffer and die because of us, foolish, sinful humans. We brought death into the world for animals.'

She looked down at Danny and continued. 'It is because of sin that animals die. But even through the sin of Adam and Eve, God is working out a good plan. The Lord never allows anything to happen for no reason. He cares about everything that happens. You know that, don't you?'

Danny looked doubtful.

'Just think of Christmas coming next month,' Mom said.

'What about it?' Danny asked grabbing a tissue.

'Well,' Mom explained, 'The only reason that we can celebrate Christmas is because God cares – cares so much that He sent His Son Jesus into the world to die for sinners. You see, Danny? God let His own Son be put to death so that there will be a new life for His children – a new life in a new world where they will never see death or sadness again.'

Mom got up and walked over to the window. 'Yes, Danny,' she said again, 'the Lord cares very much.'

PART TWO

Somehow Danny made it through the rest of that terrible day. He did his chores out of habit, then wandered out to the back field to be alone.

The next day was Sunday, and with no school or extra work to do, the time weighed heavily on Danny. The hurting inside him didn't seem to lessen. Everywhere he went were reminders of Rascal. When he pulled on his boots, he expected to see Rascal there, tail wagging hopefully to go along with him. When he walked to the barn to do his chores, he automatically kicked the ball for Rascal to chase. But there was no Rascal anymore.

That evening Dad stopped in Danny's room to tell him that they'd just heard that the driver had been released from the hospital with only minor injuries. 'Although Rascal's gone, this is still something to be thankful for,' Dad said looking at Danny.

Danny didn't answer. He felt angry inside. He felt like saying, 'Thankful? For what? That he killed my dog? He was driving way too fast!' But he was afraid that if he said anything, he might cry. And so he just turned over in bed to look at the wall. Dad didn't continue right then. He understood that it hurt. Putting his hand on Danny's shoulder, he left as quietly as he came.

Before turning out the light, Danny reached for his Bible. Opening to the bookmark, he began reading. Tonight he was at the Lord's prayer in Matthew 6. 'Forgive us our debts, as we forgive our debtors . . .' he read.

Forgive? Danny thought. Forgive that guy who was driving so recklessly? Without reading further, he snapped the Bible shut and put it away. It isn't that simple, he told himself. That guy doesn't deserve to be forgiven.

'It was an accident,' his Dad had said. 'Yes, Danny, he was driving recklessly, but it still was an accident.'

Frowning, Danny clicked off the light, then flopped over restlessly to stare at the wall, refusing to pray. He could not forgive his debtor, so he would not ask God's forgiveness. He didn't sleep well that night.

Monday, Danny had to go back to school. There he did his schoolwork as always and even forgot for a while the events at home. Three more weeks till Christmas holidays, he realized. That's why all the kids are so excited. For a moment the thought cheered him up too, but not for long. Getting off the bus after school, the loss hit him again when there was no joyful bark and wriggling dog bounding out to meet him.

At the supper table Danny was silent and sullen. Anger stewed in his heart, and bitterness was growing there. Dad tried to talk to Danny about letting go of the grief and forgiving the offender, but Danny just looked down at his plate.

Supper was finished and Danny headed up to his room to do homework. He was just coming down the stairs to get a textbook he forgot, when the doorbell rang. Danny opened the door. A boy stood there, about eighteen years old. He looked very uncomfortable. In one hand he had an envelope, and with the other he was tugging at the brim of his baseball cap.

'I, uh, are you Danny?' the boy stammered. At Danny's silent nod, he continued. 'I've come to tell you I'm sorry about your dog. I . . . well,' the boy stopped, then rushed on. 'I was going to a party at my friend's place, and well, I was driving way too fast. I didn't see him till the last minute, and then I hit the shoulder, and well,' he looked down at the ground. 'Well, the doctors say it's a miracle I'm alive . . .'

Danny just stood there and looked at the boy. So this was the boy that had killed his dog. This was the boy. Anger boiled up inside. He felt his face grow tight, and he couldn't say a word.

At last the boy looked up at Danny's white face. "But I'm guessing you wish it was a miracle your dog's alive . . .' A look of pain crossed his face.

Still Danny said nothing.

'Well,' the boy shifted his feet uncomfortably, 'I guess I'll go then. I just wanted to tell you, I mean, you deserve to be mad at me. I know what a good friend a dog can be, and I wish I could somehow, I mean, I wish it hadn't happened.' Tears came to his eyes, and he turned to go. 'Here,' he said, holding out the envelope. 'That's for you.'

Without thinking, Danny reached out and took the envelope. He watched the older boy turn and head down the front walk before closing the door. Only then did he look down at the red envelope still in his hand.

What's in it? he wondered. Money? I don't want that guy's money. Or a card? Saying what? That he's sorry? Well, sorry won't bring Rascal back. Tears filled Danny's eyes. Angrily he threw the envelope on the floor and ran upstairs with his textbook.

A little later Mom appeared in the doorway to his room. 'Who was that at the door?' she asked. In her hand was the envelope. 'I found this on the floor,' she added. 'You must have dropped it.'

'It was . . . the guy,' Danny said uncomfortably.

'You mean the one from the accident?' Mom asked and handed him the envelope. At Danny's nod, she added, 'Well? Why don't you open the card.'

With a blank face Danny opened the envelope and pulled out the card. He read it silently for a moment and then tossed it on the bed. 'I'm not going,' he said.

'Going where?' Mom asked.

'He wants me to come by his place sometime with Dad. He's real sorry and he wants to make it up to me. Well, I'm not going.'

Mom picked up the card and glanced at it. 'Well, it was very kind of him to come by. He really must be sorry. You don't have to decide today if you want to go, you know.' She turned to leave, then stopped in the doorway. 'You know, Danny, you've done wrong in your life too. For you to be able to ask God's forgiveness, you have to also forgive others.' With that she quietly closed the bedroom door behind her.

There it was again: the Lord's prayer. Forgive us our debts, as we forgive our debtors, ran through Danny's mind again and again as he tried to focus on his homework.

Nothing more was said about the invitation in the card. It seemed that Dad and Mom were leaving it up to Danny to make the first move. And in Danny's heart, the ache over losing Rascal was slowly growing less. Oh, he still missed his dog very much, but he had accepted that he was gone.

Two weeks had passed since that terrible Saturday, and today Danny went out with Dad to run some errands in town. Heading back home, Dad turned off on a side road.

'Where are you going?' Danny asked.

'Oh, I've got to stop in at the Jacksons,' Dad answered. Danny had never heard of the family before, but rode along in silence until they pulled in at a farm. Dad headed up to the farmhouse and told Danny to take a look around. 'Mr Jackson won't mind,' he said.

Danny headed over to the shed. The doors were wide open, and in the dimness he could just make out a pen fenced off in the corner of the building. He headed on over and was greeted by a chorus of whimpers and wagging tails: a litter of puppies, maybe two or three months old.

A smile crossed Danny's face as he carefully cracked open the gate. A few of the puppies crowded away from him and some ignored him, but one brave little fellow came nosing out to smell him. Soon Danny had him chasing a piece of straw along the ground.

'You can have him,' a voice said suddenly from behind.

Danny whirled around in surprise. There stood the older boy that had come to his house two weeks ago. The driver of that car. Danny jumped to his feet, letting the small pup slide to the ground. He didn't know what to say.

'I know it's not the same, a little pup instead of your old dog,' the boy went on hesitantly, 'but I thought you might like him.'

Danny looked at the boy standing there so uncertainly. He saw the apology in the boy's face and the kindness in offering him a puppy. And at that moment, he finally saw the ugliness in his own unforgiving heart, the ugliness of his own anger and bitterness. He felt shame, and once again didn't know what to say. 'I don't have any money with me,' he began.

'No, no,' the boy interrupted, 'I'm not sellin' him to you. You can have 'im if you want 'im.'

'Well,' Danny hesitated. Just then the puppy, who had been tumbling over his shoes, began tugging with sharp little teeth on his shoelace, pulling it undone. Danny laughed, and the older boy smiled.

'Thanks,' Danny said at last, reaching down for the puppy. 'And I'm sorry about, well, not saying anything the other time. I knew you were sorry, but I was just so mad still . . . Now, well, I'm glad I came,' he finished shyly as the puppy began shoving its cold nose down his shirt.

The boy smiled back. 'I'm glad you came too,' he said. 'It's hard knowing someone hates you, and that you deserve it. I . . . I prayed that God would forgive me for being so careless, and that somehow, He would help you forgive me too. And now you have.'

Looking down at the puppy in his arms, Danny at last saw that maybe Rascal's death hadn't been for nothing. Oh, he still missed his old dog and would love to have him back, but through this accident, the Lord had shown him the hardness of his own heart and the blessing of forgiveness. 🐾

37: A VISIT TO ST MARY'S

> *Therefore, brethren, stand fast, and hold the*
> *traditions which ye have been taught, whether*
> *by word, or our epistle.*
> 2 Thessalonians 2:15

PART ONE

Teresa stepped into the cool shadowy church, and Miranda followed slowly behind her. It seemed dark inside after the bright sunshine, and at first she could only see the stained glass windows with light pouring through them. As her eyes adjusted to the dim light, she saw pictures hanging between the windows: four pictures of the events during the Lord Jesus' death on the cross.

A few people were standing near the far wall, and Miranda hesitated to follow Teresa across the back of the church. When Teresa turned to wait for her, Miranda nodded in the direction of the people and shook her head.

'It's okay,' Teresa said quietly, 'Visitors are welcome, and Mass doesn't start for another hour yet.'

It was Saturday afternoon, and the two friends had been biking around the paved parking lot of Teresa's school. It was a

Catholic school, and right next door to it was the Catholic church that Teresa attended with her family. Miranda had asked why the church was open on Saturday afternoon, and Teresa had explained that if people couldn't make it to the Mass service on Sunday, they could come on Saturday evening instead.

A group of candles stood in a niche in the wall. A few of them glowed warmly on the stonework behind them, and Miranda watched fascinated as an old woman leaned forward to light another one. Straightening up, the woman dipped her head and moved her hand from her forehead to her chest and shoulders.

Puzzled, Miranda glanced at Teresa. 'She's lighting a candle and praying for someone who needs help,' Teresa whispered.

Miranda wondered why she needed to light a candle in order to pray for someone. They never lit candles to pray in her church. 'Why did she touch her forehead and shoulders?' Miranda leaned close and whispered.

'She was making the sign of the cross,' Teresa explained. 'See? From your forehead down and then across to each shoulder is the shape of a cross.'

Miranda followed Teresa as she led her down the side wall of the church. A cool white statue stood along the wall. It was of a woman dressed in a long flowing robe. Miranda could tell that she was a statue of someone from the Bible times by the cloth draped over her head. She looked like one of the women in her story Bible at home.

'That's a statue of Mary,' Teresa whispered.

'Which Mary?' Miranda asked.

Teresa looked surprised. 'The mother of Jesus, of course. Come on, we'll just go out the side door up there.'

Near the door, they passed a gold stand with a round window in it. At first Miranda wasn't sure what was in it, but after a moment the thin wafer and what looked like wine reminded her of something from her own church. The Lord's Supper. Could this be the bread and the wine from the Lord's Supper? she wondered. 'Why do they keep it in a golden stand?' she asked Teresa about it as they stepped outside.

'Oh, that's left from the Mass. You see, the priest re-enacts the sacrifice of Jesus on the cross, and the wine and wafer change into the actual body of Jesus right there on the altar. That's why they put some in the monstrance, that gold stand, because it's holy, and so that people can adore and worship the body of Jesus.'

Miranda listened silently. 'The bread and wine actually changed into the body and blood of Jesus?' she wondered to herself. 'That isn't really true, is it?'

Still blinking in the bright sunlight, the girls walked around the church to where they had left their bikes. On their way they passed another statue, almost the same as the one of Mary inside the church.

'Why do you have statues of Mary?' Miranda asked.

'Because she's the Mother of God,' Teresa said. 'Besides Jesus, she's the holiest person that ever lived. She was the only person that was born without sin and never did any sin. She's called the All-Holy One, and that's why she didn't need a Saviour. When she died, her body and soul went straight to heaven. She's there now to hear our prayers and help us know her son Jesus.'

'How do you know so much about her?' Miranda asked in surprise. She had never heard any of this teaching before.

'Well, the priest often teaches about her at our services. She is the model for us to follow – for how we should live our lives. He tells us how we should pray to her because she will protect good people. That's why she's also called the Mother of Mercy.'

The girls passed a group of statues along the side wall of the church before reaching their bikes.

'If you pray to Mary,' Miranda asked pointing back at the statues, 'then why do you have these other statues?'

Teresa climbed on her bike and started pedalling towards home before answering. 'Oh, we have statues of other saints too, because there's lots of people that you can worship and pray to. Those are all saints – really good people that hardly ever sinned. You can pray to them for different things that you need. There's all kinds of special prayers that you can pray to them. You can read them from books or pamphlets. There's prayers for the church, for your family, for a new job or a new house; for if you're in danger or sick, or dying; for studying, or travelling, or getting a new job; even for a blessing on your car.'

The girls slowed their bikes and turned into Teresa's driveway. 'Don't you just pray your own prayers?' Miranda asked as she stopped beside Teresa.

'Yeah, you can, but the church or the priests already wrote all these prayers for us to use,' Teresa said. 'Lots of people pray the Rosary every day. The pope said it's good to pray that.' Teresa held the door open for Miranda. 'Do you want a drink?'

She poured them both a glass of juice, then fetched a string of beads from a cabinet drawer. 'See?' she explained. 'This is for praying the Rosary. You start at the beginning of the row of beads, and for each bead you say a special prayer like the Apostles' Creed, or the Lord's Prayer, or Hail Mary, or Glory be to the Father. Then, when you come to the next section of beads, you announce one of the mysteries in the history of salvation before you repeat these prayers again.'

Miranda looked at the beads in wonder. She had never thought that praying could be so complicated. 'I know the Apostles' Creed and the Lord's Prayer,' she told Teresa, 'but what is Hail Mary?'

'Oh, it goes like this,' Teresa said. 'Hail, Holy Queen, Mother of Mercy, our life, our sweetness and our hope! To thee do we cry, poor banished children of Eve; to thee do we send up our sighs, mourning and weeping in this valley of tears. Turn then, most gracious advocate, thine eyes of mercy toward us, and after this our exile, show unto us the blessed fruit of thy womb, Jesus. O clement, O loving, O sweet Virgin Mary!'

Miranda frowned slightly and looked worried. 'Why don't you pray just to the Lord Jesus? He will hear your prayer. It tells us that in the Bible. And, besides, He is the one who forgives sins, so He is the one you need to believe in.'

'Yes, but Mary helps us to believe in Jesus,' Teresa answered. 'And you can't just expect your sins to be forgiven for free,' she continued. 'First you have to go to the priest.'

'Everyone has to?' Miranda interrupted.

'Yeah, well, except for babies, of course. Their baptism washes away their sins. The problem, though, is that when they get older, they sin again, so they need their sins to be forgiven again. So to get rid of your sins, you can do different things like say prayers, do penance, give indulgences, and go to Mass.'

'What's doing penance?' Miranda asked.

'Well, to do penance, you have to examine your conscience and when you're sorry for your sins, you have to be determined that you won't do that sin again. Then you go to the church and confess your sins to the priest, and do the penance that he tells you to do.'

'But if you're already sorry for you sins and confessed them and are going to try not to do them again, why do you have to do penance?' Miranda asked.

'That's to help pay for your sins,' Teresa explained. 'If you do something bad, you have to help pay for it to make it right, or else you can't be forgiven. Once you've done all this, then the priest will tell you that God has forgiven your sin.'

Miranda's head was spinning. This was all so different from what she had learned in Sunday school. Her minister and mom and dad didn't believe all this stuff, she was sure. But how come Teresa's church taught so many different things about God and Jesus and prayer? They believed in the Bible too, didn't they? They certainly had a beautiful church. In her mind, Miranda could again see the cool dim church with people reverently lighting candles and crossing themselves. She could imagine the priest walking slowly to the altar with his long robes flowing behind him. It reminded her of the stories about the Israelite temple. Somehow, it all seemed so beautiful but different and complicated. How could she know who was right?

❧

PART TWO

'Mom, can I go over to Teresa's house?' Miranda asked while covering the phone receiver with one hand. 'We want to play on her trampoline.'

Mom looked up from her sewing. 'All right, but be back for supper,' she said.

It was a cool fall day, perfect for playing outdoors. Quickly Miranda pulled on her jacket and shoes and dashed out the back door. Grabbing her bike from the garage, she pedalled around the block to Teresa's house.

Teresa was waiting for her on the driveway and led the way to the back yard. In moments they were shrieking and laughing as they jumped and flipped on the trampoline. Warming up quickly, they tossed their jackets to the ground below.

They had just flopped down on their backs to take a rest when the sliding door to the deck opened, and Teresa's grandma came out wrapped in a warm shawl. Neatly dressed and with her hair carefully styled, she still looked small and frail as she slowly carried a tray over to the table. 'Come have some hot chocolate, girls,' she invited.

When the girls came up on the deck, Teresa could see that her grandma had been crying.

'What's wrong, Grandma?' she asked, going to sit beside her at the table.

'We just heard that my sister Eunice died,' Grandma answered. Her eyes filled with tears. 'She was my only sister.'

Teresa reached over to hold her grandma's hand, and the two girls listened as Grandma told of her childhood days spent with her sister Eunice. 'We did everything together. I missed her terribly when she went away to school without me and counted the weeks until she would come back. And now she's gone again. But this time she won't come back.'

Tears ran down Grandma's wrinkled cheeks. Teresa gently squeezed her grandma's hand. She didn't know what to say. At last the girls finished the hot chocolate, and Grandma stood up with a sigh.

'Are you going to Mass this Sunday?' Teresa asked her. 'To light a candle for your sister? We'll light one too.'

'Thank you, dear,' Grandma said. She tried to smile, but couldn't. Instead she patted Teresa on the head and turned to take the tray into the house.

'I know my mom and dad will give money for her,' Teresa told Miranda as they walked over to the hammock.

'To your Grandma?' Miranda asked.

'No, they'll give money to the church for Great-aunt Eunice,' Teresa explained.

'What do you mean?' Miranda asked. 'Money for her funeral?'

'No,' Teresa answered. 'Money for her soul. You know, no one can go to heaven right away when they die – only babies and people who live perfect lives. All other Christians go to purgatory. And so we give money and light candles and say prayers for people in our family that die. Then they will be allowed to go to heaven sooner.'

Miranda had never heard of such a thing before. 'What is purgatory?' she asked while climbing into the hammock.

'That's where your soul goes when you die – if you're a Christian. You see, we do so much sin during our life that we aren't clean enough to go to heaven. So, instead, our souls go to purgatory. It's a place of fire that will make our souls pure enough to enter heaven. You might have to stay in purgatory for only a few hours, or for hundreds of years. It all depends on how many sins you have done.'

Miranda's face filled with horror. Teresa's great aunt went to a place of fire and burning? she wondered. Even though her grandma said she was a Christian? If she was a Christian, why didn't the Lord Jesus pay for her sins?

Teresa climbed carefully into the hammock next to Miranda. 'But the good thing is,' she continued, 'that people here on earth can help you be purified in purgatory quicker. They can say the Mass for you or do penance. Or else they say the Rosary prayers or give money for indulgences.'

'But what happens if you have no one to pray for you or give money to get you out of purgatory after you die?' Miranda asked. 'Will you stay there forever?'

'Yeah – no – I don't know,' Teresa answered. 'Maybe. Or maybe you will be allowed into heaven eventually after a couple hundred years.'

'And so you just try to be good so that you won't have to be in purgatory too long?' Miranda asked with a frown. 'And you hope that other people will pray for you and give money for you and stuff after you die, so that you can go to heaven sooner?'

'Yeah,' Teresa agreed.

'Doesn't that make you worried?' Miranda asked.

'I just try not to think about it,' Teresa answered.

The two girls lay on their backs, idly swinging their legs. Suddenly Miranda sat straight up. 'But don't you know about the Lord Jesus?' she asked out loud. She had seen the cross hanging in Teresa's church with the figure of a man on it. 'Don't you believe in Jesus?' she asked again. 'Don't you know that He died on the cross to pay for sin? People can't pay for their own sins by being in purgatory. Once we've broken one of God's commandments, you're right, we have to go to hell – the lake of fire. But Jesus never broke any commandments! And still He died and suffered in hell to take the punishment of sin. Why don't you pray to Him to redeem you? He'll save you and take you straight to heaven when you die.'

Teresa shook her head doubtfully. 'Jesus is God. You don't pray directly to Him; the priests do for you. Then they tell you what you need to do to be forgiven for your sins. When you pray, you can pray to Jesus' mother Mary, and she will ask Jesus to save you. But you'll still have to go to purgatory first because you do so many sins.'

Miranda listened in wonder. How could Teresa and her family believe this? This was not what she had learned in church and Sunday school. Is this an enormous lie? she wondered. She thought again of the people she had seen last week in the Catholic church. Some of them came faithfully every week to pray and light candles. And what about the priests who spent their life serving in the church? she asked herself. And look at Teresa's grandma and parents who are willing to give money and pray for their Aunt Eunice. They must believe in what they are doing.

But then Miranda thought of her own grandma. She had also lost one of her sisters this past year. She had also been very sad when she had died. But Miranda could remember the next Sunday when Grandma had come over to visit. Grandma had cried again a little, but then a smile had shone through her tears. She also had said that she would not see her sister here again on earth, but then she had added that she would soon meet her again in heaven! Hope had filled her face, and even joy, as she softly said the words to Psalter 31, her favourite song:

> When I in righteousness at last
> Thy glorious face shall see,
> When all the weary night is past,
> And I awake with Thee
> To view the glories that abide,
> Then, then I shall be satisfied.

Grandma knew that her sister had gone to live with her Saviour, and she knew that that was where she was soon going also. That is why peace could fill her face even when she cried.

Lost in thought, Miranda suddenly shook her head and climbed out of the hammock. What a difference between Teresa's church and her own. What a difference between what they both believed. It seemed that the God of Teresa's beliefs filled a person with fear of punishment, and no hope of a Saviour. Miranda would have to think more about this, but right then, she glanced at her watch.

'I had better go,' she told Teresa, 'or else I will be late for supper.'

'Just a second,' Teresa answered and scrambled out of the hammock. 'I want to show you my Bible. I got if for confirmation.' She dashed into the house and reappeared in a moment with a white Bible with a gold cross on the cover.

Miranda took it from her thoughtfully. There in her hands lay the answer, she realized. 'I think,' she said slowly to Teresa. 'I think that we both better read what the Bible says about going to hell and how to get to heaven. It has the answers about praying to Jesus, or praying to Mary. About lighting candles and giving money to the priests. About having statues in the church. And about doing confession to the priests and having your sins forgiven. Only the Bible will tell us what to believe. It is God's Word, and what He says is Truth.'

That night at the supper table, Miranda told her dad about Teresa's grandma and how her sister had died. 'Why does Teresa's church teach such different things from our church?' she asked Dad. 'They read the Bible too.'

'That's a good question,' Dad answered laying down his knife. 'You see, if churches taught only what is in the Bible, there would be far fewer differences between them. It's when churches add their own ideas to what the Bible tells us, that we get all these strange teachings. You're right, Miranda,' Dad went on. 'There is no teaching about purgatory in the Bible, and people can be saved only by believing on the Lord Jesus Christ. It is very dangerous, what the Catholic church teaches. Many souls will be lost because of their teachings. Go get the Bible a moment and read to us what it says in Galatians 1:8.'

Miranda turned to Galatians and read aloud: 'But though we, or an angel from heaven, preach any other gospel unto you than that which we have preached unto you, let him be accursed.'

'You see?' Dad said. 'No one, not even the angels, may preach anything different than what is found in the Bible. And if you read Revelation 22:18, 19, you will see that God has a terrible punishment for those who add to the Bible's teachings, or take away from it.'

Closing the Bible slowly, Miranda nodded her head. *Yes, the Bible. It held the Truth.* ✦

38: CRAZY ABOUT COMPUTERS

> *Finally, brethren, whatsoever things are true,*
> *whatsoever things are honest, whatsoever things*
> *are just, whatsoever things are pure, whatsoever*
> *things are lovely, whatsoever things are of good*
> *report; if there be any virtue, and if there be*
> *any praise, think on these things.*
> Philippians 4:8

Thump, thump, thump. Footsteps dashed up the front porch, and the door flew open.

'Hi Mom! Hi Mom! Hi!' Schoolbags dropped to the floor and footsteps flew down the hall to Dad's office.

'It's my turn! You ended yesterday!'

'Well, I got here first.'

'Hey, how come I never get a turn?'

Voices drifted back to Mom in the kitchen. In dismay, she looked at the heap of schoolbags, coats, and shoes tumbled by the front door.

'Children!' she called. 'Come to the kitchen. All of you.'

Reluctantly the children came, Steve coming last as he quickly turned on the computer. Mom got out the juice and some brownies, and pointed to the front door. 'Pick up your things and have a snack here at the table, then you can take turns playing the computer until supper.'

Pouring herself a cup of coffee, she sat down with the children. 'So, how was your day at school today?' she asked.

'Fine,' the children mumbled through mouths stuffed full of brownie. Quickly they gulped down their juice.

'How did your presentation go, Sue?' Mom tried again.

'Good,' Sue answered as she pushed back her chair. Stuffing the rest of their brownies in their mouths, the three children hurried back down the hall.

Mom finished her coffee in silence and got up to begin cooking supper.

The next day was much the same. 'Come on!' Steve called to Jake at the bus stop. 'Hurry! We'll beat Sue to the computer!'

So was the next. The front door slammed, the children gobbled down a snack, and they disappeared behind the computer until supper.

'It's beautiful out today,' Mom said the next day while the children were gulping their snack. 'Why don't you get out the basketball net and play some twenty-one?'

'Nah, I'm getting really far in my computer game,' Steve said. 'I can probably get to the next level today.'

'This is getting entirely out of hand,' Mom told Dad that night. 'All the children want to do is play computer. They have no time for playing outside, no time for each other, and no time even to talk to me! You should see them after school.'

Dad was silent for a moment, then said, 'Yeah, it's a new thing for them, computer games. It'll soon wear off, and they'll be back to their old games again.'

'I sure hope so,' Mom said with a sigh.

And so one week passed and then two.

Monday was a holiday and the children had no school. 'Look at that sunshine,' Dad said over breakfast. 'I'm going to get the yard and the gardens cleaned up, so Mom can get some flowers in. You kids can help for an hour, then get out your basketball net or bikes.'

Silence was their only answer as the children looked down at the table.

'What's the matter?' Dad asked in surprise.

'I was going to play the computer after breakfast,' Jake answered.

'Yeah, me too,' Sue added. 'I have to beat my score.'

Dad just stared at the children, then said, 'On a day like today? I thought you couldn't wait for spring and the chance to be outside again! Well, first you have to come and help outside for an hour. Then you're free to go.'

Reluctantly they nodded their heads. An hour seemed so long.

And the hour did drag by as the children dragged their feet. When Steve and Jake both wanted to wheel the wheel-barrow to the back yard, an argument broke out. Dad came around the corner of the house in time to see Jake shove Steve, and Steve grab Jake by the shirt.

'What is going on here?' Dad called out.

Quickly Steve let go of Jake's shirt, and Jake took a step back.

'You boys know better than to do that,' Dad said. 'Leave the wheelbarrow and meet me in the side yard.'

Next week, Steve had his cousin Will over after school. Mom had a snack ready for them when they came running from the bus stop. 'Why don't you play a game of Settlers or Pictionary?' Mom suggested. 'That used to be one of your favourite games.'

'Nah, Will brought a cool new game that he borrowed from a kid in his class,' Steve said. And finishing their snack, the four of them trooped off into Dad's office.

After supper Steve and Will headed to Steve's room to do some homework. When Jake poked his head in the door to see what they were doing, they told him to leave.

'Why?' asked Jake in surprise. 'I'm just seeing what you're doing.'

'Mind your own business, kid,' Will said. 'This ain't your room. If you're not gone in ten seconds, you're dead.'

'Yeah, get lost,' Steve added.

Jake's face crumpled up. He couldn't believe what he heard from his brother. Without another word, he left and slammed the door behind him.

When they had finished their homework, Steve asked Mom if they could finish the computer game. 'Will is almost at the end, and he has to give it back to his friend tomorrow,' he pleaded. Reluctantly Mom agreed.

Soon it was time to bring Will home. Dad headed to his office to call the boys. Bullets flew across the computer screen, and an opponent fell to the ground in a pool of blood. 'Ha! Got him!' Will said and clicked furiously as he moved his man across the screen out of danger. Rough language sounded as two enemies appeared.

'How many more lives do you have?' Steve asked.

'Only one,' Will answered. 'I've already used two.'

The room was silent again except for the clicking of keys. Suddenly a burst of gunfire crackled through the speakers and Will's man staggered and fell to the ground.

'Aw, you're dead,' Steve groaned. 'You didn't beat your record. Oh. Hi Dad,' he added in surprise as he looked up. He wondered how long Dad had been standing there. It was awfully quiet in the room for a moment. 'Um, this is just a spy game that Will got from his friend,' he said. 'We're getting all the bad guys.'

'It's time for Will to go home now,' Dad said, 'but I just have one question for you both. Would you feel comfortable playing this game if the Lord Jesus walked into the room?'

It was silent as the boys turned off the computer and got up to leave.

The next day Mom sent the children outside right after their snack. 'No computer today,' she told them.

'What? Why?' the children asked her.

'We'll talk about it after supper when Dad is home,' Mom said in a firm voice. The children knew there would be no more arguing.

After supper, the children sat around the table with Dad and Mom.

'Mom and I have decided to get rid of the computer games," Dad began. 'When you first asked to use the computer for games, it seemed like a harmless idea. But a month has passed, and we are not happy with what has happened. After school hours are all spent playing the computer games. No more sports outside or board games with each other. We're hearing language from you that we've never heard before, and you're becoming rough and impatient with each other.'

Dad paused for a moment and Steve spoke up. 'We're not trying to be bad,' he said. 'Maybe we're just tired of playing outside. And what does arguing have to do with computer games?'

'Well,' Mom said. 'When you spend so much time with something, it has an influence on you. The whole point of computer games is to win and become the best. This teaches you to only think about yourself instead of putting others first.'

'Yeah, but there's good things about computer games too,' Steve said. 'Like, it gives you good hand-eye coordination.'

'Yeah!' Jake added. 'You could even get a job testing video games when you grow up. You have to be pretty good at it for that.'

'And do you really think that is a good use of the life God gives a person?' Dad asked him.

Jake wrinkled his nose. 'Not really, I guess. We're supposed to serve God with our life.'

'And do you think that the Lord Jesus is honoured when we play games that use bad language and make dying seeming unimportant?'

The children shook their heads.

'You see,' Dad continued. 'After a person plays violent games for a while, the killing doesn't seem so bad. Soon you want to kill all the "bad guys" that you can. But life is precious. Every person has a soul that never dies – a soul that will go to heaven or to hell. We may never joke about dying – even if it is only on a computer game.'

'Why do people make computer games if they're bad?' Sue asked.

'To make money,' Dad answered. 'They don't care if playing the game will make children more aggressive and disrespectful. They don't care if it ruins family time. If kids will buy the games, they'll make them.'

'And so,' Mom said, 'From now on we're playing outside after school, if it's nice out. Chores will be done before supper. After supper is homework, and then you're free to read or play a game together. I pulled out Settlers, Pictionary and Sorry from the basement, and I picked up a new UNO and Checkers game, as the old ones were falling apart.'

'We'll pump up the basketball,' Dad continued, 'and set up the badminton net in the back yard. You kids can get out the croquet set, and it's time to get your bikes out again.'

᠔

Whack! 'Oh, you got me again!' Sue shouted in dismay. 'My ball went right under the picnic table!'

The boys laughed. 'You have to hit it from there!' Jake called. 'That's the rules!' And they snorted and giggled as Sue hung over the bench and swung her croquet stick wildly under the table.

Thwack! The red ball came rolling out. 'Just you wait, Steve!' she said with a grin and a gleam in her eye. 'I'll send yours under the bush!'

Mom smiled as she looked out the window. It was another crazy game of croquet. ᠔

39: ROLLERBLADES AND MISSION MONEY

> *Every man according as he purposeth in his heart, so let him give; not grudgingly, or of necessity: for God loveth a cheerful giver.*
> 2 Corinthians 9:7

The blue van door closed with a slam behind her as Vicky hopped out, her duffel bag in her hand and a knapsack on her back. This was going to be a good week. There was always lots of fun to be had at her cousin Belinda's house. Sure, they would have to help Uncle Dave around the barn and do some chores, but there would still be plenty of time for making forts in the haymow, cooling off in the pool, exploring the woods and the back fields, and just giggling late at night in bed until Aunt Joan told them to be quiet.

Belinda was just as excited to have Vicky over as Vicky was to be there. Saturday passed in a flurry of talking and biking, feeding the calves in the barn, and getting ready for bed. After whispering for another hour in bed, the day finally ended when they fell asleep. The girls awoke only when Jake, Belinda's older brother, pounded on the door.

'Get up, sleepyheads,' he hollered. 'Breakfast's ready!'
Breakfast was a table full of breads and raisin buns with lots
of tea and fresh milk.

Uncle Dave read from Malachi 3 after breakfast. Vicky didn't
really understand the chapter until he explained that the reason
why the Lord was angry with the Israelites was because they had
stopped giving their offerings to the Lord. The Lord actually said
they were robbing Him of His tithe. But, the Lord continued,
if they would bring their tithes and offerings to His temple, He
would bless them richly, so much that it would seem as though
the windows of heaven had opened and poured out blessings on
them.

Uncle Dave gave thanks for the meal and Aunt Joan
hurried the girls away from the table. 'Run upstairs and get
ready for church,' Aunt Joan urged. 'We have to leave in half an
hour.'

Pulling her Sunday clothes and shoes out of her bag, Vicky
found the roll of candy Mom had packed for her.

'Fruitellas!' she said and waved them at Belinda. Then, 'Oh
no!' she added. 'Mom forgot to give me money for the collection at church! What should I do?'

Vicky expected Belinda to say, 'I'll go ask my mom for some
collection money,' but instead, her cousin told her, 'That's
okay; I have some money you can give.'

Vicky glanced over at the piggy bank sitting on Belinda's
dresser. It was half full with money she was saving up for a
pair of rollerblades, Vicky knew. But, to her surprise, Belinda
didn't go over to her piggy bank. Instead she pulled an envelope out of her drawer and tilting it, poured some money into
her open hand.

'Here,' she said, holding the money out to Vicky, 'You can give this.'

'But isn't it your baby-sitting money, or money from doing the chores, or something?' Vicky asked, unwilling to take her cousin's money.

'Well, it was before, but not anymore,' Belinda explained. When Vicky looked confused, she continued. 'It's my church money, so it doesn't matter who puts it in the collection, you or me, as long as it goes in. See? When I didn't have a job or make any money, then I would get collection money from my mom, but now that I have some jobs, I can give my own money to the church. Well, really, it's to the Lord,' she added.

'So, whenever you get money, you just put some in your envelope to save for church?' Vicky asked.

'Yeah,' Belinda nodded. 'Not all of it, of course, because some of it I use for school stuff, or birthday presents, and I save some for things like rollerblades for the summer, but I always first put money away for the mission and church collections.'

She went over to the dresser and began braiding her hair.

'Here, I can braid it for you,' Vicky offered.

'Thanks,' Belinda replied. 'It's always easier to braid on someone else's head! But anyways, when Jake and I were old enough to start doing chores and do some work for the neighbours, we were so excited when we took our first money home. That's when my dad explained about giving money to the Lord. He said that when we grow up, if the Lord keeps on giving us strong bodies to work, we will make more money. And so, since it's the Lord that makes us able to work, and since we are supposed to help with His work before our own, we must always first give some of our money to the Lord.'

'So Jake puts away some money that he makes too? And uses it for church?' Vicky asked finishing one braid.

'Yup,' said Jake appearing in the open doorway. He had one sock on and was pulling on the other one. 'It's called tithing. We read about it this morning, you know. How the Israelites brought their tithes to the temple, except I guess they didn't use money very much back then, so they must have given ten percent of all their wheat and corn and oil and stuff, for the priests and Levites to use.'

'So you guys give ten percent of your money too?' Vicky asked her two cousins.

'Yeah, well, either ten percent or more,' Jake answered for them both. 'Dad says it's up to us. See, he doesn't force us to give a certain amount, because it says in the Bible that the Lord loves a cheerful giver. So we're supposed to give some money for the Lord's work cheerfully, to serve Him, not because Dad makes us do it.'

Vicky finished Belinda's second braid and quickly brushed her own straight hair. She was still thinking about the ten percent. 'Then, Belinda,' she finally said, 'if you made five dollars baby-sitting, you would put fifty cents or more in your envelope for church and the rest in your piggy-bank for yourself?'

Before Belinda could answer, Jake piped up from the hall mirror where he was fixing his tie. 'Yup,' he said, 'and if she made twenty dollars in a week of chores, she would give at least two dollars to the Lord.'

'And if he sold some calves,' Belinda said nodding at Jake,

'and got two hundred dollars for them, he would give twenty dollars or more.'

'That's right!' Jake said turning and galloping down the stairs. 'And if you girls don't hurry up, you're going to be late for church!'

'We'd better hurry,' Belinda said and quickly grabbed her purse and hat.

Vicky followed her cousin down the stairs, but her mind was full of new thoughts. 'Does everyone in your Sunday school class give their own tithes?' she asked.

'I don't know,' Belinda said slipping on her shoes. 'We don't really talk about it because the Lord says not to announce it that you're giving money; it actually even says in the Bible not to let your left hand know what your right hand is giving! So we don't really talk about how much money we give.'

'Oh, well, thanks for at least telling me about it,' Vicky said. 'I sometimes make money baby-sitting or weeding my neighbour's garden, but I never knew before that I should be giving money to the Lord. I guess I figured that my mom and dad gave enough money already.'

They climbed into the van where the family was waiting. 'Is there an extra collection today?' Belinda asked her dad. He nodded and told her it was for the mission. 'That works out good,' Belinda smiled at Vicky. 'Then I'll put my money in the regular collection, and you can put yours in the mission collection.'

'All right,' Vicky agreed. She thought of the money in her purse. It was not a lot of money compared to what a grown-up might give, but since it was given cheerfully and in love for the Lord's service, she knew that the Lord would be pleased with this gift. ·❧

40: THE LAST RIDE

> *Today if ye will hear his voice,*
> *harden not your heart.*
> Psalm 95:7–8

Knock! Knock! Someone was rapping on the front door.

'I'll get it!' Sam shouted and ran to open the door. A man stood on the porch, dressed in worn pants with two or three shirts layered over a sweater, instead of a coat. Sam wrinkled his nose. It looked like he hadn't shaved or combed his hair in a while, and it smelled like he needed a bath.

'Hi, there, sonny.' The man spoke in a genial voice. 'Your Dad home?'

'Just a minute; I'll get him,' Sam said, and was glad to run from the door to call Dad as well as his brother Nate.

'Hello, there, Pastor,' the man greeted his dad. 'Got any work for an honest man? I can't cut your grass like I did last summer, but looks like your driveway needs shovelling.'

'Well, now, Jed. If it isn't you again,' Dad said with a smile and a handshake. And he thought of his two strong sons who could afford to burn off some energy by shovelling. 'You know,

Jed,' Dad said aloud, 'I believe the driveway does need shovelling, and if you have the time for it, I would appreciate it.'

Sam and Nate peered from the hallway where they stood listening with their sisters. 'Yes!' Sam whispered to Nate. 'We don't have to shovel!' The two boys had finally recognized the scruffy man with the green knit hat perched on top of his head. He had come round once or twice the last two summers, and asked to cut their grass. Dad had always paid him and invited him in for a meal. To their surprise, the man had accepted the invitation.

Jed had seemed to enjoy sitting down with a family and seeing the children. He had a son of his own, he told them, but he lived in another state and didn't come home to see his dad all that often. His wife had left him, and he seemed unable to keep a job, drifting from one kind of work to the next. And so, getting desperate for money, food, or a friendly word, he would turn up now and then on their doorstep.

§

'Out you go,' Dad said to the boys as Jed headed to the driveway.

'What?' Sam protested. 'I thought you were paying him to shovel the driveway.'

'I am,' Dad said, 'and you can be glad of the help, for it's your chore.'

Sam frowned at Nate, but knew better than to argue, and soon the three of them were pushing and tossing scoops of snow into a long bank.

'You going to school, son?' Jed asked as he breathed hard with the exertion.

'Uh, yeah,' Sam answered. 'I graduate from high school this June and then I hope to get into medical school.'

'You don't say!' the older man answered. 'You know, I'd hoped to go to university myself after graduating . . . become an engineer. I had the grades for it. Even sent out my applications.'

Sam and Nate looked at the man in surprise. 'What happened?' Nate asked when Jed didn't continue.

Jed straightened up and drove his shovel upright into the snow bank. 'My Dad left and we didn't have the money,' he finally said. 'My Mom and I were still saving for school, but then she got sick, and, well, I never did make it after she died. I got married, but my wife left with my boy . . .' He stopped speaking suddenly and picked up his shovel again. 'I don't reckon you boys need to hear all this,' he said as he began to shovel once more. 'You just study hard and make good,' he told them.

Silently the boys also got back to work. With just a few words, their attitude towards this drifter had gone from condescension and disdain, to surprise and compassion.

The family was sitting down for dinner, and once again Jed had accepted the invitation to join them.

'I heard your boy there is going to med school next year,' Jed said to Dad around a mouthful of mashed potatoes. 'Good for him. He'll make something of himself, you know. He comes from a good family. He's got good parents standing behind him. It's all going for him.'

Dad continued serving the green beans. 'I don't care if Sam makes something of himself in the world's eyes, Jed,' he said as he retrieved the plate little Noelle was hiding. 'Sam will soon be sixty, seventy years old, and he'll lay his work aside. He'll grow older, just like you and me, and when he dies, he's going to have to stand before his Maker, just like you and me. Schooling and a good family and all that won't make the slightest difference then. The only thing the Lord is going to look at is our heart.'

Jed swallowed his potatoes and took a gulp of milk. 'I know, I know, Pastor,' he said. 'You've told me that before. But you've got to admit, he's got a better chance than most have, even in this salvation business. Look at the home and teaching and the parents he's got!'

Dad shook his head and sat down. 'Jed,' he said, 'Sam's starting from exactly the same place that you and I did: with a sinful, depraved, God-hating heart. He needs the same radical change in his life, and it comes from the exact same Saviour that we need – One who does not look on the outward appearance.'

The conversation turned to lighter topics as the children predicted a snow day for tomorrow with hopes of no school. Jed appeared content to listen to the family banter until after Bible reading. Then he had more questions for Dad.

'Jed, Jed,' Dad said at last while shaking his head. 'You ask a lot of questions, fair questions, but they will not get you anywhere. You were asking questions when I met you three years ago, and you're still asking questions today. You may be still asking questions on the day of your death, good questions, even. But they will not save you.'

Jed appeared to be listening as intently as the children as Dad spoke, and so Dad continued. 'I don't have the answers to all your questions, but I have told you about the one Answer that there is for the need of your soul – Jesus Christ. Don't you think it's time to stop thinking and figuring, Jed? Don't you think it's time to put those questions aside before you miss out? You need faith, Jed,' Dad said while gesturing to little Noelle, 'the faith of a little child.'

At last Jed was quiet. Everyone was quiet except the babbling baby who cooed and squealed as Mom spooned ice cream over hot slices of apple pie.

The pie was served and the family began eating. Only the clinking of forks could be heard. At last Jed put down his fork. 'That gets me to remembering, you know,' he said. And the way he said it, the children knew they were in for a story.

'Once, when I was a kid,' Jed began, 'me and my little sister went visiting an aunt and uncle of mine, and we stayed there for a few days in the summer. They took us to an old-fashioned village, a pioneer village, I guess you'd call it. My uncle gave us each a little money to spend on a snack or a souvenir or whatever we wanted. We were so excited and I held that money tight just trying to think what to spend it on; I'd never had money of my own before. Well, we were looking at home-made candles and stuff, even some neat little hand-made racing cars, but then we saw it: the merry-go-round swing thing. I had never seen anything like it before in my life. It had a shiny red roof and under the centre of it was like a puppet show with little people and characters and things popping up and down to the music.'

He stopped to take another bite. 'That's real good pie, ma'am,' he said and wiped his mouth. 'Oh, I can still hear that music, so lively and *oomphy*.'

Dad smiled at Mom. 'A real Dutch street-organ, no doubt!' he said.

'That what it was?' Jed asked. 'Well, anyways, hanging all around the edge of the roof were swings, and me and my sister watched and people got in them and when the music started and the roof began to turn the swings went too, only they started lifting out sideways from the ground, higher and higher!

'My sister went straight to the gate where a man was collecting money for the rides. She bought three tickets with her money and got on that ride and did it again and one more time.

'Boy, was she loving it. I can still see her smiling, eyes wide open and hair flying out behind her as the swings went faster and higher.'

'But didn't you go?' Noelle interrupted as Jed got a far-away look in his eyes.

'Me?' Jed asked. 'No, and that's my point. I was a little nervous. Curious and excited too. I knew I wanted to spend my money on those swings, but I didn't understand how it worked. How could those swings go up and out sideways from the roof? What was keeping them up? What if they suddenly fell in? Would I hit the puppets and music machine in the middle? What if I got hurt? And so I watched, and watched. I got in line and out of line, and when at last I got up my courage to buy the tickets, the ticket man said, "Sorry, boy, that was the last ride. You'll have to come again some other time."'

Hanging on his every word, the children's faces fell with Jed's story. What a blow for a boy who would never get another chance!

'So that was it,' Jed finished his story. 'No ride for me. I walked out of there with my sister; she was all bubbling over like with happiness, but me, I felt kinda sick with disappointment.'

Scraping the pie crumbs from his plate, Jed looked up to see a row of sympathetic children's faces. 'Well, I don't need your sympathy *now*!' he laughed. 'That was years ago, and I reckon I'm over it. Don't think I'd ride in that swing thing now even if I had the chance!' Then he grew serious. 'But what made me think of that story is what your dad said. He said it's 'time to put those questions aside before you miss out'. And he's right. I missed out once. But really, missing a ride on a swing isn't such a big deal. Right now there's something a whole lot bigger that I've just been staring at: the way of salvation.'

He stood and pushed back his chair. 'No more wasting my time on questions, Pastor,' he said. 'I've done that before, and I don't want to miss out again. Thanks for the talk and the meal, but I've got important things to attend to.'

And with that, he set his knit green hat atop his head and walked out the door.

୫

The way of salvation has been set before you too. Have you come to the Lord Jesus in prayer, or are you too busy with other things? Don't wait until it's too late.

41: RAILROAD TO FREEDOM

> *No man can serve two masters: for either*
> *he will hate the one, and love the other;*
> *or else he will hold to the one, and*
> *despise the other.*
> Matthew 6:24

Whispers passed from shack to shack in the slaves' quarters. 'Heard tell that there's freedom on the other side of the river. Heard tell that ya be a slave no longer if'n ya can make it to the other side.'

Freedom. That was a word that made faces turn serious. Most of us, we didn't know what freedom was. We were born slaves. But I knew one thing. Freedom was good. Good enough to die for. Least that's what we believed. 'Cause if you was caught trying to escape to freedom, you could die. Still, Papa and Mama and us children and the fam'ly next door and another bunch of fellers were gonna try.

It was on a dark, dark night, when the moon was smaller than my fingernail, that the conductor was to come for us. He was just a boy, a black boy like me, but free. He'd been paid for and set free. Now he lived across the river in freedom. No more master orderin' him as he pleased. No more fear of bein' sold down river away from his fam'ly. No more overseer with a whip to make him work harder. No. There was no body what could treat him badly no more, 'cause he was free.

And now this boy, this boy conductor, was comin' for to lead us to freedom. We didn't have a speck of money, an' there was no way we could ever be payin' for our own freedom. But this conductor, he knew a place where a person could be set free, an' he knew how to get there. 'Twas on the Underground Railway, he'd called it. Cross the river to freedom, then on to the North. All the way North, so's we'd never get caught.

Now you've got to realize, it wasn't a real railway we were goin' on. Nor was it even underground, my papa explained. No, the railway was a whole group of people along the way North that would help us escape. It was a system of secret trails with safe houses on the way to Freedom.

An' so there we were that dark night, waitin' on the conductor. Not all the slaves were goin' to run tonight. Some of 'em didn't be believin' there was such a thing as Freedom. An' some were just so plumb tired an' worn out that they figured they always been a slave an' they would die a slave.

But not us. No, we were sittin' in the dark of our cabins listenin' for the signal, the hoot of an owl. My throat was so thick I could hardly swallow with the tightness of it. I was sure it was the longest night that's ever been had. We were waitin' and waitin', and still no owl.

Suddenly we saw them fellers from two shacks down slippin' out into the woods. Papa stepped out to stop them.

'Ya gotta wait fer the conductor. He knows the way,' Papa warned.

'He ain't comin',' the oldest feller said nervously. 'We're leavin' on our own.'

'Don't do it,' Papa warned. 'Ya sure ain't gonna know the way to cross the river, an' come mornin' they'll send the dogs after ya.'

Restlessly, they joined us in our cabin and huddled down to wait. Had the boy conductor forgotten us? Or had our plan been found out?

Whoo! Whoo! At last. The call of the owl. Quietly we crept out to the woods. There he be: Josiah, his name. He knew these woods like the back of his hand, he said.

'Hush ya now,' he whispered, 'and follow me.'

The next few hours be ones I wanta forget. Branches scratched our faces and arms as we tried to hurry along. It was darker than pitch in the forest, and I was trippin' over everythin' that there was to trip over. And then we come to the swamp. For an hour we sloshed through muck and slime, sometimes sinkin' over our knees in water.

'This'll shake the slave-catchers when they be a-comin',' Josiah whispered. 'The dogs won't be able to catch our scent in the swamp.'

At that, the littlest one from the other fam'ly began a cryin'.

'Hush ya!' Josiah whispered fiercely to the little boy. But even his mother began to whimper.

'It's no use,' she pleaded with her husband. 'If they send them dogs after us . . . sure an' we'll be caught for certain. I'll never be seein' ya again.'

The man looked at his wife with fear in his eyes, an' even Josiah couldn't be a coaxin' them to go on. With rapid steps the small family turned back. Back to the plantation. Back to slavery.

I couldn't see Papa's face in the darkness, but I heard Mama cryin'. The other group of fellows shuffled their feet nervously. Josiah only paused a moment. Then grimly he crept on, and fearfully we followed. At last he stopped and pointed. 'We're right nigh the river now.'

I strained my eyes and squinted, but I couldn't see nothin'. A heavy fog lay over the swamp and straight ahead.

'We gotta wait for the wind to shift. Listen for the bell. It's the only way to find the crossin' to the safehouse.'

We scarcely breathed as we strained our ears to hear the bell. There was nothin'. Nothin' but the thick fog all around and the faint rush of the river. Josiah walked off a-ways, peering into the mist. Mama settled down with my little sisters, but the other group of fellers grew impatient.

'What's the matter, boy?' they asked when Josiah returned. 'Ya don't know yerself anymore where we be, do ya? Well, we sure ain't waitin' for no bell. Dawn's nigh to breakin' and we ain't bein' caught on these shores an' taken back.' And with that they moved off to some nearby underbrush. Soon they were draggin' a log down to the river's edge.

'Don't do it,' Josiah warned. 'The river be powerful strong. Wait for the bell. It'll come, and there'll be a boat to row us over.'

'Listen to the boy,' Papa also urged. 'We come this far, didn't we? Now don't be makin' your own way to cross. It's death, for certain.'

But those fellers paid him no heed. With grunts and puffs, they heaved that log right into the river and pushed off. For a moment, it looked like all was a-goin' well. But then we watched in horror as the log was caught in the current. Next thing we knew, it spun over on its side, and the whole lot of them went under. We never did see them again.

Papa clutched my shoulders so tightly I could tell his heart was achin' for the foolishness of them all. He didn't let go until Josiah came back from another look down the river. He was all out of breath this time, as though he'd been runnin' or was powerful excited.

'This way. Quickly,' he urged. 'The bell's soundin' up river.'

Like puppets, we jerked nervously after him, stumblin' in our haste. An' at last I could make out a small skiff pulled up on the river bank. Just a small flat-bottomed boat with a dark form waitin' next to it. Awkwardly we clambered in, Josiah comin' last to push us off. Strong arms took up the oars and began paddlin' us across the river.

Cold an' shiverin' from fright, we huddled in the bottom of the boat, clutchin' each other to keep steady. The river grabbed at the skiff midstream, an' for a moment my mind could see the log spinning over in the water. Every one of my muscles tensed up tight, but nothin' happened. Those powerful arms kept pullin' an' pullin'. Every stroke bringin' us closer to the other side. Every stroke pullin' us closer to Freedom.

❧

Freedom. That word has also been passed from house to house and church to church in our country. Freedom from slavery, the slavery of sin. You are one of the fugitives that have heard the news. What will be your response?

The message says to flee tonight, but perhaps you are un–believing, like the slaves remaining on the plantation. There is no way to be free of sin, is your heart's thought. Or are you so tired and worn out with fighting sin that you figure you have always been a sinner and you are probably going to die a sinner?

Flee tonight, comes the message. Are you listening? Head straight to the Lord Jesus Christ, and do not turn back. Satan would have you believe that a life serving Christ will be worse than serving him. But remember, his only wages are death, and the Lord has promised that He will never leave or forsake His people in this life and the next. Don't let your fears turn back your flight.

You've heard the message, and you're on your way. Actually, you've already escaped the clutches of sin and Satan, you believe. After all, look at the life of goodness and kindness that you live. Isn't that proof that you now have a new master?

Fugitive, beware. What skiff are you riding in? Who is paddling your boat? Are you sure you are carried by the strength of the Lord? Or are you paddling your own log across the river? Good and kind works will never save you.

The message is passed from church to church. 'Heard tell that there's freedom in the Lord Jesus Christ. Heard tell that you'll be a slave no longer if you flee to Him for salvation.'

How will you respond?

HISTORICAL NOTE: Slavery was a serious issue in America in the 1800s. Black slaves were often treated terribly by their owners, but many found comfort in their faith in God. Thousands of slaves did escape north and into Canada over the 'Underground Railway'. The remaining slaves were finally freed by President Lincoln through the Civil War.

 42: A SECOND CHANCE

> *Now unto the King eternal, immortal,*
> *invisible, the only wise God, be honour and*
> *glory for ever and ever. Amen.*
> 1 Timothy 1:17

'Mom! Mom! Guess what?' Stephanie came dashing into the house, her violin case swinging at her side. Cailyn's mom had just dropped her off at home after her Tuesday night youth orchestra practice.

'Hi, Stephanie!' Mom called from the family room. 'Take off your shoes, and come tell me what's happened.'

Breathlessly, Stephanie rushed into the room. 'Mrs Dalton has asked me to play a solo part for our concert next month!'

'Wow!' Mom exclaimed. 'That's exciting.'

'I know!' Stephanie agreed. 'I'm so nervous and excited at the same time.'

'Well, you'll have a few weeks to practise yet, and then I'm sure you'll do fine,' Mom encouraged her.

'What's this?' Dad appeared in the doorway with a newspaper in his hand. 'You're going to play a solo?' he asked.

'Well, just a solo part in one of our orchestra pieces,' Stephanie answered, but her smile stretched from ear to ear.

'That's my girl!' Dad said proudly. 'Always at the top of the class.'

'I'm not at the top, Dad,' Stephanie said embarrassed. 'There's a lot of kids who play just as well.'

'Well, Mrs Dalton must not think so,' Dad disagreed, 'because she chose you.'

Stephanie shrugged; she didn't know what to say.

The days passed and Stephanie practised her part diligently. Soon she had the piece memorized, but still she continued to practise, working on her tone and the dynamics.

It was two weeks later that a quiet Stephanie stepped out the car in front of her house. ''Bye Cailyn,' she said softly. 'Thanks for the ride, Mrs Leyden.'

Coming into the house, she set her violin case down gently on the floor.

'Is that you, Stephanie?' Mom called from the family room. 'How was practice?'

'Hi,' Stephanie answered. She walked over to the nearest chair and dropped into it.

'What's the matter?' Mom asked with concern.

'Mrs Dalton finally gave us the concert date. It's going to be on a Sunday,' Stephanie said quietly.

'Oh dear,' Mom said sympathetically. 'We didn't expect that. Your concerts have always been Friday nights.'

'I know,' Stephanie said. She shrugged. 'The tickets are ten dollars each and they're raising money for the local children's home. They want to have it in the afternoon at four o'clock so more families will come. That's right during church.'

It was quiet in the room for a moment, then Stephanie got up to put her instrument away. 'Oh well,' she said at last. 'There's nothing we can do about it.'

'No,' Mom agreed quietly. 'We must keep the Lord's day holy.'

Going up to her room, Stephanie settled in bed with her Bible. Before reading a passage, she looked over her memory work for the week. 'Now unto the King eternal, immortal, invisible, the only wise God, be honour and glory for ever and ever. Amen' (*1 Tim.*1:17). She read the verse aloud, and as she did so, the meaning suddenly became clear to her: to God must be all honour. His Name must be honoured above everything else. His wise commandments must be kept above all else . . . and He had decreed that His day must be kept holy. Stephanie's mind was full as she fell asleep that night.

The next Tuesday at orchestra practice, Stephanie told Mrs Dalton that she would not be able to perform in the coming concert. Mrs Dalton didn't seem to understand.

'I can't perform on Sunday,' Stephanie told her again. 'And the concert is right during our afternoon church service.'

With a shake of her head, Mrs Dalton hurried off into the office. In a few moments she returned with a beaming face. 'It's solved!' she said happily, 'We can have the hall for seven o'clock Sunday evening, so you'll be able to make it in plenty of time. We'll send out notices telling of the change of time and sell extra tickets at the door.'

Stephanie bit her lip and shook her head softly. 'I'm sorry, but I can't,' she said tearfully. 'I said that I can't perform on Sunday. It's the Lord's day.'

'Well, it's certainly not going to be easy to find someone to take your part,' Mrs Dalton said with a frown. She opened her mouth to say something more, then turned instead, and walked quickly to the front of the room.

The rest of the practice passed miserably for Stephanie. She could hardly hold in her tears until she got home. Then she hurried into the family room to talk with Mom.

'She seemed pretty angry,' Stephanie sniffed, and Mom put her arm around her shoulders.

'Well, you did what was right,' Mom encouraged her, 'and the Lord has promised that He will honour those that serve Him. His honour must come first, not our own.'

Just then Dad came walking into the family room. 'How's my star?' he asked loudly. 'Showing them all how it's done?'

When Stephanie didn't answer, Dad looked from her tear-streaked face to Mom's sober expression. 'Hey! What's going on here?' he asked. 'You didn't get kicked out, did you?' he joked.

Stephanie swallowed but couldn't seem to answer.

'The concert is going to be on a Sunday,' Mom told him softly, 'so Stephanie can't play.'

'What's this?' Dad bellowed. 'That's ridiculous. Of course she can play. Don't go putting ideas in her head.'

Stephanie looked from Dad to Mom. She was ready to cry again. 'No, Dad,' she said. 'Mom didn't put ideas in my head, I just told Mrs Dalton myself. Sunday is the Lord's day, and we have to keep it holy.'

With a fierce scowl, Dad threw his newspaper down to the floor and left the room.

'I wish Dad would come to church with us on Sundays,' Stephanie said and curled up against Mom's side. 'Then maybe he would understand.'

That night Stephanie curled up in bed with a book. She needed to read a chapter each night in order to get it finished on time. At school her class was writing research biographies, and she had chosen to do her topic on Eric Liddell.

Eric Liddell was born to missionary parents in China, Stephanie had found out. He lived there in China until he was five years old, then moved to Britain with his brother to live in a boarding school for sons of missionaries.

Even as a boy, Eric was an amazing athlete. In school, he was always top in sports and especially in running. Eric practised hard, and soon he became known as the fastest runner in all of Scotland. He found that he could serve the Lord in his running, for when his school sent him out to run races for them, he was also expected to give a talk to the spectators afterwards about his Christian faith.

In all of his success, the Lord kept Eric from becoming proud. The headmaster of his school said that Eric never showed any vanity over his great talent.

When Eric went to university, he focused on running the 100- and 220-yard races. Soon Great Britain wanted to send him to the Olympic Games which were being held in Paris in 1924. Scotland had never had a gold medallist before, but with Eric running, they felt they had a chance. Eric was willing to run for his country, for he said that running was a talent given to him by God. He loved to honour his Lord by preaching and by running.

But when the schedule came out a few weeks ahead of the races, Eric found out that the heats for the 100-metres race, his best distance, were to be held on Sunday. 'I cannot run on Sunday,' Eric said. Many of his team-mates and coaches were not happy with his decision and tried to change his mind, but they could not. And so Eric spent the last few weeks before the Olympics practising for the 400-metres event instead, which would not be held on a Sunday.

The day arrived, and Eric ran the 400-metres race. He not only won the gold medal for his country, but broke the world record with a time of 47.6 seconds. Eric returned to China the next year, and although he continued to run races occasionally, he spent the rest of his life there as a missionary. God used him again in this way to bring honour to His name by teaching the Chinese about the Lord.

᠅

It was the Friday before Christmas, and the concert hall was nearly full. Music filled the air as parents sat beaming up at their children performing on-stage. Small children wiggled restlessly in the audience as the orchestra came to its last piece.

The conductor raised her baton, and once again instruments were lifted into position. 'Peaceful and slow,' the conductor reminded the orchestra quietly, then gave an encouraging smile to the soloist standing to the side.

For a moment the room was breathlessly silent. Then the baton dropped, and all the instruments came in together. The sound grew and filled the room, and for a time there seemed to be no violins, violas, cellos and basses – just one voice pouring out in song.

Stephanie waited, motionless, then lifted her violin to her chin. As the sound of the orchestra faded away, all eyes turned expectantly to her. Smoothly she raised her bow and drew it across the strings. Notes soared from her instrument and filled the air. Her eyes shone calm and clear, and each finger took its place as the hours of practice bore fruit. And when the last note died away, the faces in the audience were shining too, caught up in the beauty of the melody.

For a moment there was silence, then a rush of applause filled the room. Suddenly Stephanie saw Dad stand up, still clapping. With a grand rustle, the rest of the audience joined him. Bursting with happiness, and only now feeling her shaking knees, Stephanie quickly bowed and sat down. Mrs Dalton turned to face the audience, and the rest of the orchestra rose to take their bows.

'That's my girl,' Dad said proudly as he met Stephanie in the hall. He held her violin case while she got her coat. 'All those hours of practice, and you showed them what you can do.'

'No, Dad, it's not me,' Stephanie said, buttoning up her coat. 'I only put in the practice. God gave me the love for music and the talent.'

Standing beside Dad, Mom smiled quietly at her. 'You did very well, dear,' she said. She squeezed Stephanie's hand as they stepped outside. 'Unto Him be all the honour.'

43: KING OF THE JUNGLE: PRINCE OF THE EARTH

> Be sober, be vigilant; because your adversary
> the devil, as a roaring lion, walketh about,
> seeking whom he may devour.
> 1 Peter 5:8

The sun is setting over the open grasslands. Golden rays of light outline the few scrub trees scattered along the horizon. A group of elephants slowly leave the swampy river's edge and tramp off through the grasslands into a small brush area. In the distance, a herd of buffalo shuffle around, keeping close together while they settle down for the night. Everything seems peaceful and still as the last light of the sun fades completely away.

Soon darkness creeps over the land, and even the natives that live here head to the safety of their homes for the night.

For we are in eastern Africa, and this area along the river is called Tsavo, an African name for 'the place of slaughter'.

Slowly the moon rises, casting a faint light on the earth below. Gone is the scene of golden grass and peaceful wildlife, for with nightfall come new movements and sounds. No, it is not the cheerful chirp of the cricket or the comforting croak of the bullfrog that we hear, but instead the quiet rustling of grasses. It almost sounds as if something is passing very closely by us. We hold our breath, and . . . over there!

A dark form glides through the grasses, its tawny coloured fur blending in perfectly with its darkened surrounding. 'A lion!' we breathe softly in terror. His muscles ripple under the smooth skin of his shoulders and back, as he lopes easily up a small rise in the ground to our left. Thankfully, we are upwind of him, and he does not sense us.

He pauses there on the small hill to check his surroundings, king of the night. The lion's remarkable senses by night give him an advantage over animals that he dare not face by day. Weighing 180 kilograms, he relies on his strength and cunning, more than his speed, to bring down his prey. We watch him and hope that he doesn't catch wind of us, for although the lion isn't one of the fastest animals in the grasslands, he can still run twice as fast as any human sprinter. We could never outrun him, we realize, or even outclimb him, for lions can climb trees.

Soon the group of buffalo catches his attention, and the lion waits, studying the layout of the group. He has grown hungry through the day, and nightfall has brought his hour – the hour of the hunt. As a rule, he focuses on prey that are numerous and vulnerable. He hunts for animals that travel in groups and will attack those that stray to the outskirts of the group.

The lion grows restless now, and hunger drives him forward. Opening his mouth in a snarl, we can see in profile his huge canine teeth; the base of each tooth is about the size of a Canadian dollar. His snarl, far louder than a hissing house cat, opens wide into a roar. A boastful sound of such cruel intent and danger, his roar sends our hearts into our throats. Sweat stands out on our foreheads, even though the night is cool, and we clutch one another's hands so tightly that they hurt.

The buffalo are alerted to the lion's presence now and shuffle uneasily around in their group, keeping a watchful eye on the great beast. By day they would not fear him, for their powerful horns can do great damage, but they know that the night is his, and they fear. Stealthily, the lion slips down into the long grasses once more and begins creeping towards the buffalo. His tail flicks slowly from side to side as he watches with pale yellow eyes between the blades of grass.

Like a shark, the lion circles his prey. Nervously, the buffalo sidestep and turn from him, huddling into their group. The lion picks up speed, singles out a lone buffalo a few metres from the group, and explodes into a strike. At the last possible moment, the lone buffalo sees him and, startled, leaps off into a panicked flight across the grasslands.

We watch horror-filled as the lion springs after it in hot pursuit. Legs churning, the two animals speed across the grasslands. The lion does not gain on the buffalo, however. He had miscalculated his attack, and should have crept a few feet closer before springing.

Soon the lion slows to a lope as he realizes that he is losing his prey. He is not willing to waste more energy on a useless chase. As a hunter, he relies on his strength in wrestling down a victim, and so he hunts by ambush, not by chasing down other animals. Ah, he missed this time, but defeat is something he will not admit. The hunger inside him drives him to go on. He will spend the night on the prowl. Licking his lips, he lowers his head once more in a snarl, and creeps off through the long grasses, seeking whom he may devour.

The natives of Tsavo have lived in this area all of their lives. Many people here have lost their lives to lions, and that is how the area came to be named 'the place of slaughter'. The Tsavo natives would have shaken their heads in warning to us, if they had seen us out in the grasslands at night. The lion is not an animal to be taken lightly. He is an enemy that we need strong defences against.

୫

Satan is also compared to a roaring lion, going about, seeking whom he may devour. As a lion brings down and devours his prey, Satan also tries to capture people, dragging their souls down to hell with him. He comes with temptations; temptations to sin.

The first person Satan ever attacked was Eve in the Garden of Eden. 'Hath God said, Ye shall not eat of every tree of the garden?' he asked her. This question was like the swipe of the lion's paw, as he tried to catch his prey. And in this case, it worked. Eve fell into sin, and then Adam did too.

From that day on, Satan has been busy walking about the earth like a roaring lion on the hunt, seeking whom he may devour. If even Adam and Eve fell to Satan's temptations, how can we escape this great enemy?

Notice what Paul says at the beginning of our text: 'Be sober, be vigilant.' This means, be watchful, pay attention!

Just as the lion circles the group of buffalo looking for a weak point to strike at, Satan will tempt you when you're tired, when you're having too much fun doing things your own way to think about serving God, when you're least expecting it, or when you have been lazy in prayer.

We must be watchful, and also ready to fight these temptations. In their letters, Paul and James give advice on how to counter the attacks of Satan. You will notice that these verses begin with help from God, before telling us what we must do. Paul tells the Christians: 'Put on the whole armour of God, that ye may be able to stand against the wiles [cunning traps] of the devil' (*Eph.* 6:11). And James says: 'Submit yourselves therefore to God. Resist the devil and he will flee from you' (*James* 4:7).

And lastly, the words of Jesus Himself to His disciples, are: 'Watch and pray, that ye enter not into temptation' (*Matt.* 26:41). For there is no one better to call on for help than Jesus. He is the One who defeated all of Satan's temptations.

43: THE SUBSTITUTE

> *For Christ also hath once suffered for sins,*
> *the just for the unjust.*
> 1 Peter 3:18

A hard look crossed the farmer's smile-lined face. 'It ain't right,' he said shaking his head. 'A man spends his life in honest, hard work, and some young upstart comes along and ruins it. Thanks to him, I've lost a week doing repairs, and I've got no place to let my cattle out to pasture. If it hadn't been for the rainstorm that came up, I could've lost the whole farm . . . and who knows how far the fire would have spread! It's been a dry summer and some of you could have lost your farms too.'

Several of the neighbouring farmers were gathered in front of the hardware store to discuss the recent excitement. Having finished his long speech, Farmer McKinlay stood and slapped his hat against his pant leg. 'When I catch that young hooligan, he's going to pay for this,' he added.

'You gonna teach him a lesson?' one of the men suggested. 'Give him a lickin' that he'll never forget?'

'Nope,' McKinlay said firmly. 'He's going to clear me a new pasture. He ruined my back field and cost me and my son

238

a week's labour. I figure he's going to clear me a new field out behind the south pasture; it'll cost him a good week's labour.'

The farmers looked at each other. Didn't seem so bad. A few honest days' work in clearing out the underbrush, though there were a couple of trees to take down too. Hard enough work for even a man, but then those teenagers always seemed to have energy enough for trouble. Let them burn off some energy by swinging an axe for once. But suddenly Farmer Dowsett spoke up. 'Say, ain't that all one great big wild berry patch growing back there?' he asked the older man.

McKinlay pressed his lips together and nodded his head soberly. 'That's right. A nasty berry patch. But the trouble-maker should've thought of that before he went and set my field on fire. Now that new pasture's got to be cleared. I have no place to set my cattle out to graze until it's done, so I'll give him a week to clear it.'

The neighbouring farmers looked at each other. Some raised their eyebrows, but most grunted their agreement. That would teach the young ruffian. Crime had to be paid for, and it was well that the severity of the punishment matched the serious-ness of the crime.

❧

Micah pedaled hard, hurrying past the McKinlay place on his worn bicycle. Farmer McKinlay's son was outside, repair-ing one of the fences that had been burned in the fire. He spotted Micah and straightened up to wave. Micah nodded his head in return, wishing there were another road that led home. It wasn't that he didn't like the older boy. No, quite the opposite was true. Although he was old enough to have finished school, Jason was a boy who still had a smile and friendly word for the younger children. Not one mean word about anyone had Micah ever heard from Jason's lips. How could Micah not admire the older boy who worked so hard, missing out on the amusements of the other young folk as he spent his evenings helping his ageing father on the farm? And he still managed to find time for others, for wasn't Jason the one who had taught Micah to shoot a slingshot, pegging off crab apples clear across the field?

Micah tried to shake these thoughts from his mind. They only made things worse. Why, oh why, had he joined the motley group of boys in town? he asked himself. They were bigger than him, older than him, tougher than him, and, oh, he had wanted so badly to fit in. To have a group of friends. To be one of the crowd that walked down Main Street Friday night, laughing and elbowing each other. Not to be the skinny, short kid hurrying along by himself . . . Yes, that was why he had done it.

'Well, go ahead,' the older boy had said as the others looked on. 'You wanted to become a Viper, well, take the dare.' And with a deft motion he lit the torch and held it out to Micah.

Pale and freckled, Micah's white face stood out in the growing darkness, his dark hair disappearing against the bushes they were crouched behind. Initiation into the group? He had wanted it, and he had got it with a vengeance. He stared aghast at the torch flaming brightly before the older boy's mocking face. Somehow . . . in some way . . . he had hoped it was all a joke, a test to see if he would show up at the field.

Even now, he was still half-expecting the boy to stamp out the torch, slap him on the back, and welcome him into the band of Vipers. But no such thing happened. The torch continued to flicker against the darkness, burning with deadly intent. It was now or never.

Still pedalling feverishly, as if to distance himself from the deed, Micah closed his eyes tightly against the memory. He could still feel the roughness of the homemade torch as he had suddenly seized it from the boy's hand and, closing his eyes, hurled it into the farmer's pasture. 'There! You see? I did it,' he said boldly, but the other boy had already gone. Grasping his bike by the handlebars, Micah too, had yanked his bike to the road and taken off, the eager flames lighting the field behind him.

Why, oh why had he done it? Micah asked himself. How could he have been so foolish – so wicked? And now Farmer McKinlay had announced his punishment. The news had spread through the farming community like wildfire. And, somehow, the group of boys that he had been so eager to join seemed rather too eager to tell him every bit of news and hints, real or imagined, that McKinlay was on his trail. The Vipers certainly weren't standing behind him the way he had expected they would.

Threats and hints and suggestions ate away at Micah and he couldn't sleep the night following the deed, or even the next. His throat carried a lump so big that it wouldn't allow any food past, and he grew thinner and paler. Even his mother who usually paid him no mind, frowned at him. 'What's the matter, boy? You going to get sick on me, or something?' she demanded. 'Eat your supper.'

Micah could only shrug, and when five days had passed since the night of initiation, he knew that he could carry the weight of guilt no longer.

§▪

The farmer's son opened the door. A small form stood black against the darkening sky, and a reedy voice faltered, 'Is . . . Mr McKinlay . . . home?'

'Sure,' Jason said and stepped back opening the door wide. 'Come in,' he welcomed, gesturing to the pool of warm light that spilled from the kitchen. The farmer was seated at the table with a newspaper, and the clatter from the sink told of dinner dishes being washed by his wife.

Fumbling with his laces, Micah pulled off his shoes. He steadied himself against the door-jamb before walking on shaking legs to the kitchen.

'Yes, my boy! What can we do for you?' Farmer McKinlay was all friendliness as he lowered his newspaper.

Micah opened his mouth to speak, but nothing came out. He swallowed hard, and tried again. Still nothing. Unwanted tears rose in his eyes, and Jason reached out to give him a friendly pat on the shoulder.

'Hey there, Micah; it's all right. What did you want to talk to my dad about?'

Micah shrank away from the friendly hand and began edging back to the door as he tried again.

'I'm the one . . . who . . . set the fire,' he choked out at last and braced himself for the angry outburst.

The crinkle of the newspaper was the only sound as slowly, carefully, Farmer McKinlay closed the paper and folded it neatly on the table. His eyebrows drew together as he looked at the boy standing before him, young and thin, nearly white with fear. He was, perhaps, twelve years old, but so delicate-looking that the farmer didn't suppose he could wield an axe for more than an hour before giving way. This was certainly not the brash, swaggering ruffian he had expected to ferret out. What could have possessed such a meek youngster to commit such a rash, unprovoked, and dangerous act? Slowly, McKinlay pushed back his chair. It was pure folly, it was; a damaging wickedness that would have to be paid for.

When the silence grew long, and the farmer did not immediately get up, the boy opened his mouth as though to speak, but once again, nothing came out. Jason watched as he passed a trembling hand across his mouth in a nervous gesture. It was a thin, pale hand, one that was not accustomed to physical labour.

At last the farmer rose from his seat and walked around the table. Folding his arms, he leaned against its edge. Some things, at least, were clear: the cattle needed new pasture land, and the underbrush had to be cleared. He had made it known that this crime would not go unpunished, and the culprit was standing before him. Justice was held dear by the old farmer, and he would have the whole town see that sin would reap its reward . . . and, yet, . . . mercy was also dear to the old man's heart, and it was clear that this boy was not able to bear the punishment.

A heavy sigh finally broke the silence as Farmer McKinlay turned to his son. A silent conversation seemed to pass between them. The son at last looked away from his father and walked to the window that opened south on the burnt pasture and the uncleared brush beyond. Turning back to the other two, his eyes rested briefly on Micah's small form before meeting his father's steady gaze. 'I'll do it,' he said firmly.

§.

A miserable rain was falling, the kind that soaked your hair and ran in rivulets down your neck. Still, some of the town kids had come out and gathered along the fence to jeer at Jason. 'Just look at you now, so high and mighty! The farmer's own son! How does it feel to do a real's man work for once?'

Jason seemed to turn a deaf ear to the taunting as with bleeding hands he hacked and tore at the thorny underbrush and piled it into a wagon. For three days now he had been at work, and with much of the field yet to be cleared, Jason was rising with the sun and working late into each night. Yesterday had burned hot with sunshine and today was soggy with rain.

Standing off to one side, Micah clenched an angry fist at the other boys' mocking. Oh, they saw the humiliation in the farmer's own son bearing his father's public punishment, Micah thought, but didn't they at least see the honour in Jason himself? In his willing sacrifice?

How dare they! Micah stormed inwardly as a boy shouted an especially cruel taunt. But as Jason raised his head and looked past the boys to where Micah stood alone, he nodded his head in his old, friendly greeting. Shame and remorse filled Micah at the brotherly love the older boy still had for him, and he paused in his angry thoughts. *How dared the other boys?* No, he was the one at fault here, for *how had he dared to commit such a crime against such love?*

TOPICAL INDEX